Little Luke's

Big Heart

Little Luke's Big Heart

A Witty Guide for Loving a Medically Fragile Child

David Chisholm

Unless otherwise indicated, Scripture quotations are from the Holy Bible, New International Version®. NIV®. Copyright © 1973, 1978, 1984, 2011 by Biblica, Inc.™ Used by permission of Zondervan. All rights reserved worldwide. www.Zondervan.com

Cover Design: Wayne Joiner
ISBN: 9781072628903

To Lucas, the one who continues to light up the world for me and everyone around him.

Contents

Introduction

O n December 17, 2008, my pregnant wife Rachael and I heard a doctor say the words, "There's something wrong with your baby." Nothing is more terrifying, heart-wrenching, or life-changing than those words! We searched long and hard for a book that could help us, and while there were a plethora of books and stories to read about suffering kids, nothing I could find at the time offered much in the way of advice, or direction, for navigating our own difficult journey. A book like this would have been useful as we learned how to navigate hospitals, therapies, and the monumental challenges of raising a special needs son. As a result, I primarily offer the following chapters to families who have experienced the heartache of learning that there's something seriously wrong with your kid. It sucks, and nothing's going to magically fix it, but hopefully, this book will help you through tough times.

The secondary audience for this book is anyone who has ever had the opportunity to come alongside a friend or family member who is walking the "now what?" road and would like to know how to help. We all want to be Christlike and minister, but how do we actually do it? This is tricky territory. I'd like to provide a little illumination by telling you what it was like for us—what we found helpful and what we didn't. I would also like to give you whatever small insights I possess on ministering to people in this particular kind of crisis.

I suppose I'm also selfishly writing this for my two children, Luke and Sam. They may someday want to better understand what life was like for our family as we went through all of this. While Rachael and I sought to make their childhood as normal as possible (whatever that means in a world in which celebrities get to be president and teenagers are eating Tide-Pods on the internet), "normal" was never really in the cards for them. Perhaps, they may gain a little perspective from reading about the early years of our family after they have grown. Chances are, I won't leave them a large pile of money (tell all your friends to buy a copy of this), so hopefully reading the ramblings of Dad will be cheaper than the therapy they will probably need. Ironically, their mom *is* a marriage and family therapist, but there are rules against therapizing your own family; not that this has stopped her from trying to therapize me (but that's a different book). So, all of that to say, Luke and Sam, I hope this manuscript proves helpful, or at least mildly interesting to you.

Don't worry too much about the chronology of what follows. I wrote most of the events in this book in the order they happened, but sometimes it made sense to deviate for thematic reasons. Also, it took several years before I was in a place to write this, so I don't always remember everything perfectly (shocker). These are the events, conversations, and characters as

Introduction

I remember them. There are a few theological excursions as well. I can't help it; I'm a preacher at heart.

I'm giving fair warning at the outset. This book will be a different kind of book—mainly because I think I'm funny. I'm not interested in writing some serious tome on suffering, or a deep, theological work that's only interesting to preachers. If you want something heartfelt to cry over or something with heavy theological chops, I can give you several good recommendations from authors far more serious than I am. As you press deeper into this book, I hope it will cause you to laugh while it also makes you reflect on something quite serious. For a TV analogy, I'm aiming for something like *Scrubs* (not season 9—we'll just pretend that one never happened), or perhaps *MASH* for the senior citizen readers. (Yes, I just called you old.)

Everyone has plenty of burdens, drama, pain, and suffering in their own world, so the last thing you need is to vicariously take on any of mine through this book. I apologize in advance for anything I wrote that comes across as harsh, lacks empathy, or steps over the line from funny to mean. I hope you will laugh and receive encouragement as you travel through this story. You can be the judge of whether I succeed. A wise preacher recently said, "Journeying with God is more a trek through the desert than it is a walk in the park." Okay, so I preached those lines last week, but I still think it's true, and it's easier to type that than look up something inspirational from Gandhi, Oprah, or Yoda.

Blessings,
DC

CHAPTER 1

The Best Laid Plans

Have I not commanded you? Be strong and courageous. Do not be afraid; do not be discouraged, for the Lord your God will be with you wherever you go.

Joshua 1:9 NIV

I like a good plan. I know of preachers who, lest they quench the work of the Holy Spirit, will write nothing down prior to giving a sermon on a Sunday morning. They believe in spontaneity, living for the moment, and embracing the sense of adventure that is life. Some of you (mostly the youngest-born of the family) resonate with that. Your dream vacation would be to just get in the car, hit your playlist titled "adventure groove" (or something else equally asinine), and hit the open road with no agenda. That would drive me absolutely insane. I'm the kind of preacher who likes to have my full sermon written and my slideshow properly formatted by Thursday afternoon. It would terrify me to preach if I didn't already know where I was going. As for vacations, those should be planned, organized, and kept to a reasonable level of adventure. My wife, Rachael, is more spontaneous than I am, but she's also more organized, so we work really well together. We're both laid-back middle children who appreciate keeping drama to a minimum and highly prioritize peace and harmony (we're basically awesome).

So, Rachael and I had a superb, keep-adventure-to-a-reasonable-level, promote peace and harmony, plan when we decided to do life together. We planned to graduate from college before we got married, so we graduated one weekend and got married the next. We planned to attend graduate school together, so we moved to Abilene, Texas, and did our respective programs simultaneously. After that, we wanted to go straight into church work, so it excited us to learn I had a job lined up immediately upon graduation. I finished my master's degree in December 2007 and started my first career-job preaching for the Rockwall and Brin Church of Christ in Terrell, Texas, on the first Sunday of January 2008. The church also provided a great place for Rachael to hang her shingle and start a therapy practice. Our reasonable and peaceful life-plan was well laid out. We had found a church crazy enough to hire a 24-year-old preacher. We were close enough to our extended family without being too close (an important place to be by the way), and we were finally ready to start a family.

We intentionally didn't want to have kids until we had a good full-time, full-paycheck job. I've always worried too much about money, so one thing Rachael and I wanted was to make sure we had at least one stable job between us before bringing home our own little bundle of joy. We also waited because we witnessed the struggles other couples still in school endured because they had children early. Under the best of circumstances, kids are hard! You can ask any parent who has ever seen hands reaching under the closed bathroom door or witnessed a meltdown because a sticker isn't sticky anymore, or played the game, "is it chocolate or poop?" if kids are hard, and they will be all too happy to share with you some horror stories of their own. But we had a plan, and a stable job, and we were as ready as we were ever going to be. So, we started trying to get pregnant.

*Note to the reader—skip this next paragraph if you don't want to read about baby making!

Like a lot of couples, we had a few months of nothing. And, like most couples, after a few months of only seeing one blue line on the pregnancy test, we started to think worst-case scenarios. "What if my swimmers aren't swimming?" "What if her womb is a barren wasteland?" "What if we aren't doing 'IT' right?" And within this time period is the awkwardness of having your wife consult a day-planner and an article she read on WebMD in order to decide on the best days and times to seduce you. I mean, I'm a guy, so it's not like I would say "no", but still, it takes the romance out of it when you figure out your wife isn't so much interested in your rugged manliness as she is in the ONE step you can contribute to creating life. It's a good step, but still, I'm not just a piece of meat.

Finally, one day Rachael thought it might have worked. She took a pregnancy test, but was too excited to look at it, so I got to see it first, and

I knew. There's something about seeing that second blue line that takes your breath away. You've prayed for it, you've been working towards it, and you're expecting it, then suddenly your world expands.

When I got married, I became responsible for my spouse, but it's not the same as having a baby. Pre-baby I made decisions with Rachael in mind, but I know she's a capable woman who can take care of herself when she needs to. In a marriage, we're responsible for each other, but neither one of us is helpless. Suddenly, with a baby, this new life totally depends on us.

A little context on this, I have an older sister who was very interested in a career and other things, and so she chose not to have children. I also have a younger sister who would have children later, but she wasn't ready for the having babies' stage of life yet. On Rachael's side, it was a similar story. She has an older brother who didn't desire children and a younger sister who would later have kids. All this to say, when Rachael and I finally became pregnant, this baby became the first grandchild on BOTH sides of the family. That's a big deal! I don't remember the reactions of everyone when we told them we were expecting, but I'm reasonably sure the happiest I've ever heard my mother was when we told her she would be a grandma. She even informed me she already picked out her grandmother name, "Gigi."

Pregnancy was a little scary. It was a lot exciting. We had a lovely and reasonable dream to have our family. We were now expecting baby #1, and everything was going *exactly* as planned.

The Best Laid Plans

~

When I was a teenager, my youth group took an annual trip each summer to Six Flags Over Texas. The joke I'd make a few years later as I was working on a preaching degree was that if you flip over any youth minister's degree you would find a map to the nearest Six Flags. I thought it was funny. My youth minister friends didn't. Now, as a teenage boy, one of the highest goals in life is to avoid any situation in which people will think you are scared, weak, or incapable. This goal is quadruply important if teenage girls are watching. So, on this particular youth group trip, I determined that I would ride whatever the other teenagers wanted to ride even if it meant getting on a stupid, big, fast, scary, why-did-I-come-on-this-trip roller-coaster. Of course, the first ride my group of friends wanted to get on was a roller-coaster with a nice big double loop at the bottom of a 900-foot (I might be guessing here, but that seems about right) death plunge. I still remember shaking as I climbed into the seat, but the part I will never forget is the sinking feeling in the pit of my stomach as we slowly climbed the first hill. As the death-machine hit an almost free-fall down the other side, my stomach felt pure, unadulterated fear. I survived the experience, and would eventually come to love roller-coasters, but that feeling (shot of adrenaline, ice in your veins, terror, almost passed out, uncertainty of survival, gut-punch) stuck with me for a long time.

The story above is the closest parallel I can think of to the feeling I had when we got a level two sonogram on December 17, 2008. We went to the doctor that exciting day looking forward to finding out whether we should paint the nursery blue or pink. You say you'll be happy with whatever you're having. Somewhere deep down in your heart though you're secretly hoping it's a boy, so you won't have to face the day when your teenage princess comes to you in clothing too revealing and declares that she has a boy coming by to pick her up for a date. (Okay, don't hold that last line against me. I have zero experience with a daughter, so I'm admittedly trotting out a completely sexist stereotype to make myself feel better because I wanted a boy. Don't email me.) We spent the extra money to get a tape of the sonogram. After all, who doesn't want to watch a video of a fuzzy blob over and over again? The tech turned off the lights and started her thing, and I was absolutely thrilled beyond what I could have imagined to learn we were having a little boy. Visions of playing with action figures, baseballs, violent video games, and Star Wars Legos flashed gleefully through my mind.

What came next was the gut-punch. You know how a lot of parents say, "I don't care what we're having *so long as he/she is healthy*"? I understand why parents say that, because ultimately, it's your kid, and you will love your kid no matter what. The highest hope in your existence at that point becomes for your child to *thrive* in life. What you really want in your heart of hearts is not a specific gender, but a healthy baby. Stop and read that last sentence again. All you want is a healthy baby. Unfortunately for Rachael and me, the doctor came in on the heels of the sonogram tech and told us there was a problem with our baby. Gut-punch. He saw on the screen that something was wrong with our baby's heart. Part of it hadn't formed correctly. In a daze, I heard him say our next step would be to drive to another hospital where we could meet with a specialist who would hopefully see us immediately to give us more information.

Have you ever had one of those times in life in which only seconds go by, but the moment itself was so intense that it stretched on for what seemed like an hour? Maybe it was as you got up in front of a crowd to make a speech or the moment when the preacher asked, "Do you take this woman…". Maybe it was when you watched your kid fall off his bike for the first time. You saw him heading for the pavement, but there was nothing you could do to stop it. Time stands still. As the doctor told us our baby was not okay, I literally felt the blood drain from my face. It honestly felt like someone punched me right in the stomach. Before I fell over, I had to sit down.

Only one other time in my life have I had that sit-down-NOW feeling. It was the day our second son, Samuel, was born. After all the drama of Luke's life, I felt relieved to have such an easy, low-stress baby experience. When it was time for Rachael to get her epidural, I knew I could handle it, no problem. I was an old pro with medical experiences at this point. I've seen things. Dang it, I'm a man! Then, this "doctor" took out what looked like a soda straw and calmly stuck it right into Rachael's spine as I watched. For the second time in my life, I had to sit down before I fell down. Note to future fathers—DON'T WATCH THE EPIDURAL.

Back to our story. I eventually made it through the initial shock of hearing the worst words a parent could ever hear. I stood back up, held my wife and our baby inside her, and we cried.

Little Luke's Big Heart

~

Several hours and another sonogram later, we were sitting in the office of a fetal-cardiologist (I didn't even know there was such a thing) as she explained that our son had Ebstein's Anomaly. This means the little valve that regulates blood flow between the two right side chambers of the heart had not properly formed. Instead of blood flowing from the top chamber to the bottom chamber and then out to his lungs, our baby had a lot of blood that just flowed from the bottom chamber straight back up to the top chamber. That's bad. There are only two real options with this condition. You can either get a heart transplant (not a great plan), or you can reroute the entire circulation system through a series of three open-heart surgeries over the course of about three years. This effectively bypasses the entire right side of the heart. This option doesn't sound much better, does it? Typically, pregnancies with this condition have about a seventy-five percent chance of successfully carrying to birth. With our particular kid and the way his heart ballooned in his chest, the chances didn't look great. We walked out of the doctor's office that day knowing there was a decent shot our kid would never be born alive. In our best-case scenario, if he *was* born alive, we faced years of surgeries and medical procedures, and the rest of his life would be largely defined by his medical condition. Gut-punch. From that moment forward, we were heart baby parents, and life would never be the same.

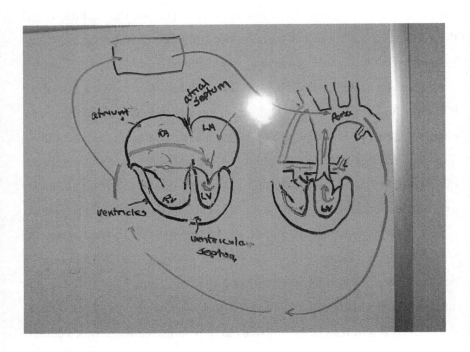

The whiteboard where Luke's surgeon walked Rachael and I through Luke's first heart surgery.

CHAPTER 2

When Bad Things Happen to Good People

The Lord gave and the Lord has taken away; may the name of the Lord be praised.

Job 1:21b

A lot of academic knowledge which teachers delight in pouring into students seems completely inconsequential until you run into a real world, suddenly consequential, situation. I had to take a totally lame typing class in high school, but it wasn't so lame when Blizzard released *Diablo 2* a year later (pre-headset days). Suddenly, I needed to type quickly at other players as we liberated the world of Sanctuary from the vile clutches of Diablo and his minions.

Little Luke's Big Heart

Many computer mice died for this worthy cause. Typing was lame, then it became valuable. Math works the same way. You don't care about fractions until you've got four friends and three doughnuts. Poetry didn't matter to me until my junior year when a cute blonde girl asked me if I wanted to go to a poetry reading. She was a senior so of course I did. (That's not relevant to the story, I just want you to know I was a junior dating a senior.) She turned out to be crazy, so my love of poetry lasted for the same two weeks as our relationship, but you get my point. We often learn stuff in life where only later do our experiences dictate the true value of that knowledge.

This applies to our present story because when I was in seminary I worked as a graduate assistant for an Old Testament professor, Glenn Pemberton, who regularly taught on the wisdom literature of scripture. His teaching on the book of Job was particularly helpful, as he deconstructed what I thought I knew and then reconstructed something deeper, richer, and more meaningful. I always took good notes when Dr. Pemberton taught because, as a wanna be preacher, I knew that in the not too distant future, those notes would provide invaluable material as I crafted my own Bible classes.

Fast-forward to December 2008. On the day everything in our lives changed because of a life-threatening diagnosis for our baby, I was prepared to go teach a Wednesday night Bible study on...you guessed it, the book of Job. Suddenly an academic Bible study wasn't so academic anymore. Suddenly one of the most uncomfortable and misinterpreted books of scripture became the material of my life.

At this point, I would encourage you to pause, grab a Bible, and go read the book of Job. Yes, I know full-well the probability of you going right now to read 42 chapters of wisdom literature is about the same as the probability that I'm going to make a hole-in-one the next time I play golf. It *could* happen.

So, here's the synopsis. Job is super holy and is the greatest man in the East. (I don't know who held the western title.) He is so holy that he regularly offers sacrifices for his kids just in case they might have inadvertently sinned the day before. Not only is he Mother Teresa-level holy, but he's also Bill Gates-level rich with ten kids, thousands of cattle, an army of servants, and at least one loving wife. Things are magnificent for Job.

Next, we get a glimpse into the kingly courtroom of God. Here, God and the Accuser are having a conversation about Job in which the Accuser claims that if all of Job's blessings and riches disappeared from his life, then Job would chuck his faith (aka, curse God). The story then proceeds to tell us how Job loses everything; all his kids die, his servants leave, thieves plunder his cattle, and his wife even encourages him to curse God and die. Job's story is the ultimate riches to rags story, and we've only gotten through chapter 2. We've still got 40 to go—if you're counting—and I think by this point, we can already see the primary question driving this entire book: If a person's blessings are taken away will they keep their faith in God, or will they leave it? The book of Job is not about answering why bad things happen to good people, it's not about explaining anything about how Satan works, nor is it explaining suffering (more on all that later). It's a question of faith. When the bottom falls out of life, do we stick with God? This book applies to us not because we are either super-righteous or super rich, but because at some point the bottom will fall out of our lives, and in that season, we have to decide what to do with our faith. We believe in a God who is big enough to rescue us from our suffering. So, what do we do when he doesn't?

The next major characters we encounter in the book are Job's friends, whom I believe honestly wanted to help their buddy out. They tell Job three things. I give one scripture reference per point, but his friends repeat these multiple times:

1. Sinful people suffer (Job 20). This is common knowledge. Everybody can point to numerous examples of times they have seen sinful people reap what they sowed.

2. Since you are suffering, you must be sinful (Job 22:1–20). If everybody knows that sin leads to suffering, then the logic is simple. Judging by the enormity of your suffering, Job, you must be sinning on an *epic* scale. We might not see the bodies, but we know they are buried somewhere.

3. Repent (Job 22:21–30). The good news is that we serve a loving, merciful God. If only you would repent of all these dastardly sins, Job, then God would forgive you and even bless you again. All you need to do is confess your sins, and God will happily come near to you once more. Life can be good again, just repent Job!

All in all, that's not terrible advice. It's certainly better than Mrs. Job's advice to curse God and die. In fact, the idea that blessings go with holiness and suffering goes with sinfulness comes straight out of earlier sections of scripture (see Deuteronomy, which is the theological prequel to Job; also, see a bunch of the Proverbs which say the same thing). The problem with the friends' three-point sermon is that life doesn't always work that way. Our lives are much more complicated than a mechanical formula.

Job quickly responded with his own theological trifecta:

1. Sinful people don't always suffer. In fact, sometimes they do quite well (Job 21:1–16). We've all known powerful, wealthy people who thrived at life, and yet they were awful people. This may be news to you, but sometimes (rare occasions, I'm sure) wealthy, powerful people get to be wealthy and powerful *because* they lie, cheat, and steal their way to the top.

2. I'm not dastardly. Job does not deny his integrity throughout the entire book. In chapter 27:1–6, he emphatically declares, "I will not deny my integrity." Here, Job is blasting apart the logic of point number two from his friends. Sometimes suffering happens when it's not linked to a specific sin.

3. LET ME BE UPSET (Job 7). Because everyone knows that when you have a friend who's extremely angry or upset, the best way to calm them down is to tell them, "Calm down." (Insert your own marriage joke here. I've been married long enough to know to leave this one alone.)

At several points in the book, Job speaks directly to God (Job chapters 9, 19, 23, 24, and 31 to name a few). A better preacher might enumerate a more nuanced list than this, but I believe Job basically says two things to God:

1. God, you need to be more just. Or another way to say it might be, "God, I don't deserve this suffering." We're all cool with wicked people suffering, but the faith crisis happens when the suffering falls on the wrong

people. Nobody's perfect, but everybody can see the injustice of kids starving in a third-world country or wives being beaten by drunk husbands. There are victims in the world who just flat don't deserve it. Job didn't deserve it.

2. Arguing with you is pointless. Job knows arguing with the creator of the universe is a losing proposition. Even if Job is right and God is wrong, (not really a thing) then who's going to come alongside Job and vindicate him? Who gets to judge God? God holds all the cards in every encounter, so arguing with him is like going "all in" after the river card when the five cards on the table are better than the two in your hand. For those of you more righteous than I, who don't know Texas Holdem, I'm saying you can't win. Job voices his objections to God with the full knowledge that it's a losing argument.

God finally answers Job at the end of the book. By the way, if you're only going to read one section of Job, let it be chapters 40–41 because they're *epic*. God basically makes only one point, but being God, it's a good one. Out of a mighty storm, God thunders, "You're not God. (Full stop.) You complain about justice and fairness, but who gets to define justice and fairness? Who do you think you are? I'm the creator of the universe, and I don't have to explain myself to you." The one overwhelming point God unleashes before Job is... I'm God, and you're not. Like I said, good point.

Quick wrap-up: In the final chapter of the book, Job whimpers, "Okay God, you're right." Notice 42:3, in which Job says, "Surely I spoke of things I did not understand, things too wonderful for me to know." Then, God explicitly condemns the advice from the friends, vindicates Job, and gives Job even more blessings than he had before. Yet again, Job gets 10 more kids, double his thousands of cattle, and goes on to live a long, full life. Yay, Job!

All right, I have a couple of points about this last chapter of Job. In the first place, there have been numerous occasions in my life in which I really would have liked God to come down in a voice of thunder, condemn my opponents, and vindicate me. (Anyone who's been in church leadership meetings has in all likelihood prayed for exactly that.) Secondly, and more importantly, just because God blesses Job at the end of the story, he doesn't exactly make up for the losses. Sure, he could replace cattle, but Job lost *ten children*. I don't care how many more kids he had, he'd never get over the loss of his first ones. So, does Job have a happy ending? Kind of. But I still think, overall, the book is not about Job's blessings at the end. It's about a righteous man who didn't deserve all the bad things that happened to him, and despite overwhelming pressure, *he kept his faith*. The book doesn't answer all the questions I have about suffering, but I feel it answers the most important one. What should I do when the bottom falls out of life? Stick with the God who brought me here in the first place. Many practical applications exist from this great wisdom text, but before those, we need another story break.

~

Now that I've reached my mid-thirties, I'm embarking upon a quest to stay young. I know "young" is relative, and some of you will hear mid-thirties and think, "You're just a young pup getting started! Back in my day...*grumble, grumble, grumble...*" For others of you who are younger, mid-thirties sounds like, "Oh, I had no idea. I'm sorry for your loss. Do you need help with your smartphone?"

A few months back I got a new (to me) car—my first with Bluetooth connectivity. I mentioned to my youth minister (a young twenty-something) that I hadn't spent a lot of time using Bluetooth. Without even thinking about it, he smarted off, "I guess that makes sense *for your generation.*" So, I fired him on the spot, went home, yelled at the neighbor's kids to get off my lawn, and ate dinner at 5:00. I'll teach him to call me old!

So, I'm doing things to try to stay young. I quit drinking three (or more) sodas a day; I exercise some; I am more diligent about my sleep, and in general, I'm trying to take care of myself. But my body betrays me. Back in my early twenties you might call and invite me to a 10 PM movie and I'd be all in. Now if you ask me to do something and I won't be home until after 10, yeah, you can just tell me later how it went. I kept the same waistline from age 17 to age 31. Since then I've gained twenty pounds. A while back my barber said, "Wow, you've got more gray than when I first cut your hair." You know what old man? I don't pay you for the commentary. I mentioned a few of these things to my dad, and with great pastoral encouragement and abounding sensitivity, he said, "Ha! Just wait until you get to be my age." Yep, I know that no matter how diligent I am in my desire to stay young, no matter how many Cokes I cut, or how much sleep I get, it's a quest destined to end in failure.

My somber point is that the quest to stay young is actually the wrong quest. The real quest should be to live out however many days I've got left (maybe forty or fifty years for me, but any of us could go tomorrow) in the best way possible. If the quest is about staying young, then not only will I consistently fail as I age, but I'll also drive myself crazy. Just think about the vanity of the old lady who knows her plastic surgeon better than she knows her grandkids or the old man who thinks he's fooling *anybody* with that comb-over. I don't want to be comb-over guy (or face-lift lady for that matter). I want to age into the cool old dude who lives in each season of life with grace and dignity, making the most out of every opportunity.

Okay, forgive my metaphor because I know it breaks down at some point, but the quest to stay young is like the quest to answer the big suffering question "Why?" Why is this bad thing happening to me? Why is this tragedy happening to my kid? Why would a good God, who could fix this if he wanted to, allow this suffering? The quest to answer the "why" question, much like the quest to stay young, is not only the wrong quest, but it will drive you absolutely insane.

When Rachael and I learned something was terribly wrong with our baby's heart, I desperately wanted an answer to the "why" question. Maybe I had done something wrong? Could this be my punishment for a sin I committed? I knew I wasn't the most righteous man in the world like Job was. I hadn't helped the poor and oppressed nearly as much as I should have. I had consumed "entertainment" that Christians shouldn't consume. I talked to people in ways I would never want them to talk to me, and I could certainly go on. I've got a long list. I get it, I'm a sinner. But I feel like I'm fairly normal in the sin department (not making any excuses), and normal people don't consistently watch their children simply struggle to live.

Little Luke's Big Heart

As a Christian, I know I'm a sinner, but I also know I'm forgiven. It's bad theology to think I'm going through this particular suffering because of something I did or neglected to do. Again, there are times in my life in which I suffer and can point to the exact sin that got me there. If I mess up in my marriage, I don't have to wonder why I'm batching it on the couch. If I speed by the policeman, I can be fairly certain why I got a ticket. If you ever say, "Hold my beer and watch this!" then you deserve whatever happens next. But when a child is born with a heart valve that didn't form properly, there's nothing I or anyone else did that caused it. In suffering, looking for the sin is the wrong quest. Please read the last sentence again (and again) until you believe it. I've done a lot of pastoral counseling and seen many people get stuck here. For most of your suffering, looking for the sin that caused it is the wrong quest.

It's also important to point out that God is not a monster. If God was punishing my son with a life-threatening illness because of something bad I had done, then that would make him a monster completely inconsistent with the picture of the loving father we read about in scripture. I firmly believe God loves me, abounds in mercy towards me, wants what's best for me, and would do nothing to harm me. Read the Prodigal Son story in Luke 15 if you need a better picture of God as our father to hold in your head. I repeat, God's not a monster.

Let's go back to the book of Job. Job isn't seeking to answer the "why" question, and honestly, not much of the rest of the Bible answers it very well either. What Job does is give us a better quest: How should I live out my faith when I get gut-punched by life? At some point in your life, you will very likely go through something traumatic; you'll lose a spouse, lose all your money, lose a relationship, or lose *something*. Sometimes these tragedies come to us in groups, as they did for Job. I don't know what the trauma will be, and it may be more than one thing. What I do know is that when the bottom falls out from under you, it will force you to make a faith choice.

The first choice we can make with our faith is to chuck it. We can curse God and be done with it. It's interesting to note the book of Job never tries to blame Job's suffering on Satan, or Job, or anyone else. God is God. Whatever else you believe about him, if you believe in God at all, you believe God could have stopped whatever you are going through. He didn't. So, the first logical option is to chuck your faith.

The second choice we can make with our faith in suffering is to lean into it. Since I live in the South, I rarely drive on ice, but I'm told the best thing to do when spinning on ice is to turn the wheel into the spin rather than fight it. It's counterintuitive, but it's actually the best way back to normal. (BTW, don't be that guy who comes to the South and says, "Well, I'm from the North, and I know how to drive on ice. None of you southerners can do it like we can up North." NOBODY likes that guy. There's a phrase we could use to talk about you, but my mom might read this, so I can't print it here. Don't be that guy. And bless your heart.) My point is that when you lean into your faith in suffering, it won't answer all your questions, and it won't always feel right, but it's the fastest path back to wholeness.

Once we decide to lean into our faith, then the one point God makes in Job (I'm God, and you're not) becomes a word of comfort. If God is right (seems like a good bet to me), then that means I don't have to answer the "why" question. It's no longer my question to answer. Why was my son born with a heart defect? I don't know. More importantly, I don't have to know. I'm not God. A big part of what living by faith means is that I don't have to know everything. I believe God does, and I'm going to trust he will do whatever he needs to do with that knowledge. Maybe someday it will all make sense. Maybe it won't. Either way, God's big enough to handle it.

~

Before we move on with the Luke saga, I've got to give you the bigger picture. Reading Job in isolation is kind of like watching one of the middle *Harry Potter* movies by itself. It tells a good, complete tale, but it makes a lot more sense if you know how it fits into the bigger story. The bigger story of *Harry Potter* can't be over until the seven Horcruxes are destroyed and Lord Voldemort is finally defeated (spoiler alert). The bigger story of scripture, of which Job is a middle piece, is a story with four major acts, and it can't be over until we've come full circle.

Act One: God created a perfect world.

Without getting too deep into the weeds, Genesis contains two different (I think complimentary) stories of creation. Chapter one opens with a poem describing seven days of creation in which God fashions order out of chaos, and we repeat the refrain "God saw that it was good" often. And this "good" is stronger than the way we typically use the word. When God says it's "good" he means it reflects God's own perfection. Genesis two then gives us a narrative in which God creates a perfect, pleasing Garden of Eden in which he places Adam and Eve. Again, it's an image of perfection with a garden to supply every need, everyone's running around naked, and everything is all good. Unfortunately, act one doesn't last very long.

Act Two: Sin, death, and chaos wreck the perfect world.

In Genesis three we get the infamous story of eating the forbidden fruit (insert your own "she started it" joke here). From that moment on, God's perfect creation is no longer good. Sin, death, and chaos run rampant throughout the world, and people go from bad to worse.

Act Three: God makes a covenant.

In Genesis 12, God speaks to Abraham and makes him a series of promises. We call these promises The Covenant. Most of the rest of the Bible will be about how God will keep these promises even though people suck (that's the technical, theological term for it). And I'll skip the next fifteen centuries (give or take), but everything ultimately leads us towards Jesus who will finally fulfill the Covenant and truly begin the process of fixing the brokenness of all creation. Long story short, God keeps the covenant even though people don't.

Act Four: Restoration.

People who are Jesus' followers get to be a part of God's plan to restore all of creation. As Jesus' followers, we get to see some of the restoration happening now in our own lives, and in the world around us. This restoration won't finally be complete until Jesus comes back and makes everything "good" again like it was back in Act One. The story ends at some point in the future when God will restore all of creation.

Little Luke's Big Heart

There's a reason the first book, Genesis, begins with a garden scene and the last book, Revelation, ends with a garden scene; we've come full circle. What this big, circular story means, is that we, like Job, live in a world still awaiting its final restoration. We live in a broken world. Bad things sometimes happen in a broken world, and it's nobody's fault. So, while some of our sufferings directly correlate with sinful or stupid things we do, some of our pain and anguish is nothing more than the result of the fact that we live in a wrecked world awaiting the final restoration of God. Babies have heart defects. Loved ones pass away. Storms rip through peaceful neighborhoods. Whose fault is that? Nobodies. We live in a broken world. The good news of scripture, and the reason Christians live with hope, is we know brokenness will not get the last word. Someday God will fix all of it. God will destroy even death itself. Someday even broken hearts will be put back together again.

So will it be with the resurrection of the dead. The body that is sown is perishable, it is raised imperishable;

I Corinthians 15:42

CHAPTER 3

God Gives the Best Gifts

I prayed for this child, and the Lord has granted me what I asked of him.

Hannah—I Samuel 1:27

Once a year in Oklahoma all the plants decide to put out every single grain of their pollen all on the same day. (I know nothing about plants, so it may not *really* work like that.) I vividly remember one particular time in college during one such allergy season when it felt like I breathed in every. single. grain. Traditional allergy medications seemed about as effective as eating a Skittle, so someone suggested I try Benadryl. At the time I didn't know and was in too big of a hurry to read the package that would have told me, but Benadryl causes drowsiness. So, first thing one morning, I popped two

Benadryl and headed off to my first class. I then proceeded to lose an entire day to the fog of medication. My body went through the motions it should go through; I went to class, worshiped during chapel, ate lunch, suffered through some more classes, and eventually made it home, but I was aware of very little of my day.

That same kind of going-through-the-motions-fog is exactly what it was like for Rachael and me as we continued through the days following Luke's diagnosis. I continued to preach sermons and teach classes each week. We cooked meals, did laundry, and watched movies. I know we continued to do the normal activities of life, but none of those actions got my full attention, and I absolutely, positively, definitively, *did not care*. I couldn't care. I remember going to my parents' house in Oklahoma for Christmas a few days after the diagnosis. While there, my dad and I played golf just like we always do, but I remember thinking how absurd it was that I was playing golf while our baby's diagnosis never left my mind. To be fair, golf is something of an absurd game in which grown men exaggerate about how well they can hit a little white ball. It's also expensive, and harder than it looks—not to mention that I still can't beat my retirement age dad. I went ahead and played golf through the fog, zombied through the motions of each day, and settled in for the worst Christmas present ever. It's the most ridiculous thing in the world to play games when all you can think about is how you are waiting for your child to die. I played, but I simply didn't care about golf or anything else right then.

God Gives the Best Gifts

~

I feel like it's important to note here that, much to my wife's dismay (she's mostly over it now, I *think*), I don't like the whole process of gift-giving. I mean, sure, if you walked up and handed me a stack of Benjamins or the keys to a new car, I'd love it. (March 8 is my birthday, FYI.) However, there are two things I don't like about gifts. The first is the gap that exists between what the giver imagines the gift is worth and the relative value of the present in the recipient's life. I'm thinking about a nice old man from church who once gifted me with a Bible in a translation I will never read. It's a beautiful, genuine leather Bible, has my name imprinted into the leather (so I can't return it), and I know it cost him a considerable sum. Unfortunately, it sits in a box in my office, and I can count on one hand how many times I opened it. He thought it was a lavish gift. I certainly appreciate his thoughtful, loving intentions, but the value of that present in my life is less than a Butterfinger—which is indisputably the best candy bar. You can have a different opinion on this theological candy-point, but you'd be wrong. I know, I know, I know, "it's the thought that counts," but the next time you're giving a gift, ask yourself if you'd be okay with the recipient thinking a candy bar would be more useful than the expensive gift you are about to give them, but hey, at least they'll appreciate the thought. Also, you know as well as I do that right now you can think of gifts you've gotten where you were thinking, "No, you *really* shouldn't have."

The second thing I don't like about gifts is the way they create obligations. Let's imagine you were blessed enough to be my co-worker, and my birthday rolled around. (Remember, it's March 8.) To help me celebrate, you purchased a present for me that cost $50. Let's also imagine you did an excellent job of reading me, and I value your gift at the same $50 you paid for it (perhaps it's a case of Butterfingers). Great! Except, in addition to giving me a present, you've also given me homework. Now I am obligated to give you a gift on your birthday. Not only do I have to make sure I properly mirror your gift, but I also have to risk getting you a $50 gift that ends up relegated to some future garage sale or gathers dust somewhere because you feel guilty about dumping it. I can't get you a $25 gift or you'll think I'm cheap, and if I get you a $200 gift, you'll feel bad about the gift you gave me. *Best-case scenario,* if everything works out perfectly, we swapped fifties, and we created a whole lot of hassle. I know my gift feelings are quite jaded, but somewhere deep in your soul, you know I'm right.

The ultimate exceptions to my gift-giving feelings are the gifts we get from God. He knows better than we do what gifts we really want, so there's no chance of us using one of his gifts as a dust collector. Also, God gives gifts *freely.* There's nothing we can give back to God that would ever match what he's given to us. When God gives gifts, all we can give back, and all he wants, is praise. Turns out my creator is good at giving me gifts, so while I'm not a big fan of gift-giving, I'm a huge fan of accepting gifts from God.

So maybe it's a coincidence or maybe it just happened to work out this way. Maybe, but on Christmas Eve, while we were waiting for our miscarriage, Rachael felt Luke kick for the first time. Suddenly he was more than an extra blue line on a pregnancy test or a blob on the sonogram screen. Suddenly Rachael felt *life* within her. Our baby was moving. Even with his oversized heart and all the complications that went with it, our child was growing and kicking. We knew we might lose him any day, and we still had a long way to go, but it certainly felt like God was giving us a Christmas gift at a time we desperately needed it. It was the gift of hope and life, and it was more valuable than I can describe. We needed a reminder that if our baby would survive to birth, it would be by the grace of God, and he wasn't intimidated by the odds against us. So, maybe there was no gift, and it was just a coincidence we felt our baby move on Christmas Eve. Maybe. But Rachael and I know better.

~

Our baby continued to grow over the following weeks, and the number of doctors' appointments steadily increased. Then one day we went for yet another sonogram, and our usual doctor, a wonderful man named Dr. Rosnes, wasn't available, so a different doctor from the same practice came to check on our progress. I'll never forget his name, but I won't share it with you for fear I'd be maligning the name of a #$%&**& doctor still tormenting patients somewhere in Texas. This doctor, who *worked with pregnant women*, had a bedside manner equivalent to a butcher handling cuts of meat. He was probably competent at the technicalities of his job, but he wasted no time considering the feelings of whoever was on the table in front of him. I know that sounds harsh but read the next paragraph before you judge my metaphor.

Little Luke's Big Heart

This new doctor spent a few moments looking at our baby's heart on the sonogram. Then, in the same tone of voice you would use if you were predicting rain this weekend, he said, "Oh yeah. This heart isn't going to make it. You might carry him for a while longer, but this one's bad. Every once in a while, you'll see one like this survive to term, but I'd be surprised at this one." Then without so much as asking us if we had any questions, he left to, presumably, go see his next victim. Apparently, for him, the oath to "do no harm" had nothing to do with the emotional or mental health of expecting families. The only good part of this story is we never saw that particular practitioner of pain ever again.

This side note is to any doctors who might be reading this. You may have seen a hundred cases exactly like this one, but remember, this is a first for us as patients. You might forget about us in ten minutes, but we have to live with whatever you say and the way it comes out for the rest of our lives. More on doctors, most of whom were great, in a later chapter.

What followed over the next few weeks was excruciating. We were waiting for our baby to die. Every time Rachael felt him move, we celebrated. She spent all day, every day, counting kicks. Every time there was a significant gap between movements, we feared the worst. The absolute worst time came when one day she did not feel him kicking at all. She didn't panic at first and tried all the usual things: drank orange juice, jiggled him, drank something cold. Nothing worked, and the sinking feeling of finality hit both of us. We called her OB and started the drive to confirm that we had lost him.

On that day three distinct thoughts went through my mind.

43

God Gives the Best Gifts

1. This sucks worse than anything I've ever known. I don't know how people made it back in olden days when the childhood mortality rate was about fifty percent. Maybe they were stronger back then, but I don't think I could handle losing half my children.

2. I will have to be Superman for Rachael now. As bad as I was feeling about losing our child, nothing compares to the feelings of the woman who carries a baby, feels the life inside of her, and literally has that child as a part of her. Maybe it sounds sexist to modern sensibilities, but moms are wired on a different level than dads are. Rachael would need me like never before after this.

And 3. This is the hard one. I feel some shame associated with this, but I write it hoping it will help someone who reads it. This confession is one of the worst ones I will ever make in my life, but a part of me thought it was good that this would finally be over. I knew it would be better for us to lose him now rather than later or, heaven forbid, after he was born and we grew to love him more. I knew that as hard as it would be to lose him, it might just as easily drag on for months, and then we would lose him. Lots of people have lost babies, grieved, and been able to move forward with their lives. We would cry our tears, but we would have other children. We would look back on this day as a hard day (maybe the hardest day), but not as the end of our story.

As you've doubtless guessed (since there's more to this book), the OB got out her little thingy (that's the medical term for it I believe) and heard his heartbeat. We hadn't lost our baby after all. The next few months steadily marched on, and our baby continued to grow. For a baby who wasn't supposed to live long enough to be able to survive birth, he eventually made it to over 38 weeks and shocked us all. Two things I know. God still gives the best gifts, and doctors can be wrong.

~

There is a certain order in which you're supposed to do things in life. You should watch Star Wars episodes 4 through 6, then episodes 2 and 3, and then you can watch 7 and the following films. (Notice how I left out *The Phantom Menace*? Yeah.) You're supposed to graduate from high school before you go to college, and you really better drink a cup of coffee in the morning before you have to talk to people. If you get these things out of order, it can really mess you up.

Well, in having-a-baby-world, you're supposed to go get your level 2 sonogram, find out what you're having, and then you get to do the fun parenting thing of picking the name you want your child to carry with him/her for all time. Steps one, two, and three. Don't mess up this sacred order.

There are relatively few things for which I'll actively judge people. For the most part, I know everyone has their struggles, so if you're addicted to crack, I assume it started innocently, and I won't judge you. If you're an ex-con who robbed a few banks back in the day, I'll assume your home life was rough, and I won't judge you for that either. But there is a short list of things that lead me to believe you deserve all the judgment I can possibly heap upon you. I judge people who treat dogs like children. I judge people who like Pepsi over Coke. I judge people who take the wrong number of items through the express lane at the grocery store. And

I especially judge people who give their kids stupid names. "Oh, we named her Chrysanthemum because we just LOVE floral arrangements." I judge you! "We named him JackTom, all one word, because we wanted to name him after both of his grandfathers." I judge you too. If you only get one thing out of this book, let it be this: *Don't name your kid something stupid!* I know you want your little precious to be unique, but please, let your child's uniqueness come from his or her developing personality, not from something that sounded cool to you while you were watching *Game of Thrones*. Naming a kid is important! End of rant.

So, one of the odd things that happened to both Rachael and me when we found out there was a strong possibility our baby would never be born alive was we didn't want to give him a name. We didn't talk about it with each other to make some sort of well-reasoned decision about it, it just happened. It sounds horrible now, but at the time, we both instinctively felt we shouldn't name our baby. This illustration is crude (honestly, as a preacher I make illustrations for a living, as hard as it might be to believe after you read what's next), but you know how parents of kids who grow up on farms don't let their kids name the pigs, cows and chickens? You know why, right? It's so when Wilbur is on the breakfast table as bacon, you can eat him and not feel like a monster. I warned you it was a terrible illustration, but eh, people better than you have judged me. The single biggest reason we didn't want to name our son was that we were bracing ourselves for the next doctor's appointment, or the one after that, or the one after *that*, in which we knew we would get the dreadful news our baby had died. I know it's silly and makes little sense, but somehow giving him a name would hammer home to us that this life we created was indeed our son. We were bracing ourselves for the loss. So, for quite a while, we didn't name him.

Then one day we were in for a checkup back with the fetal-cardiologist. She was a lady we ended up loving so much that if our second child had been a girl, her name would have been Jane after this doctor. She asked us about our baby's name. We sheepishly told her we hadn't named him yet. I don't know if she had seen this so many times that she knew what we were doing, or if she sensed this was a need we didn't know we had. Maybe she was just tired of writing "baby Chisholm" on the chart, but for whatever reason, she encouraged us to name our son. I'm glad she did.

Something that's not at all that unique to our situation is that naming a kid is more difficult than it seems like it should be. Obviously, any name shared by one of Rachael's ex's was out. Any name one of our close friends has used for their baby is out. Baby name stealing isn't really a crime, but I'm told that to women it's socially on par with manslaughter. Also, when you're naming a kid, it quickly becomes apparent that there's a long list of people you don't like. Ryan was the kid in 4th grade who bullied me, so not only will I not name my kid Ryan, but if I run into you and your name is Ryan, I'm automatically going to flinch just a bit. Nothing personal. And if the kid will *ever* attend middle school, you have to think about what dirty words the kid's name might rhyme with, sound like, or get shortened to. I actually like the name Richard, but just, no. I still remember a kid in school who had the last name "Peters". I always felt bad for that guy. Side note, churches should employ one of the middle school boys to proofread anything they will put on the church sign, in the announcements, or out to the general public for any innuendo. If the thirteen-year-old boy giggles when he reads it, it needs editing. If you don't have a middle school boy handy, use the youth minister. Add to all of that, Rachael and I wanted his name to have real meaning, so naming him something that sounded good but meant nothing wasn't an option.

We debated over several names but finally settled on Lucas with the plan of calling him Luke. In the first place, it's the name of one of the four accounts of the life of Jesus from the Bible. History even tells us that Luke, the author of The Gospel According to Luke, was a doctor, which would be appropriate for our medical kid. In the second place, the name itself means 'bringer of light', which carries all sorts of cool parallels for the life we wished for him. In the third place, I knew that someday his kindergarten teacher would read through a list of names, and while she or he was struggling with all the Chrysanthemums and JackToms, she would have no trouble with "Lucas". In the fourth place, and not least important, I would always be able to say in my best James Earl Jones impression, "Luke, I am your father!"

We had a baby. We had a name. Now we just needed him to grow a bit longer and get here.

CHAPTER 4

She's Having a Baby

I praise you because I am fearfully and wonderfully made;

Psalm 139:14a

A handful of days in your life will be transition days in which you know nothing will ever be the same again. The day you get your driver's license. (Freedom!) The day you graduate from school. (More Freedom!) The day you get married. (Okay, not exactly freedom, but I was so happy she agreed to marry me that I didn't care.) The day you become a Christian. (Which, not for nothing, the Bible talks about as a new birth.) And of course, the one day absolutely everything changes in your life, even under the most normal of circumstances, is the day your first child is born. And if you don't have kids, don't try to tell me about how your precious dog or adorable cat is like your kid. (Yup, I'll judge that one too!) I don't care how much you love them, how fuzzy-wuzzy-cutesy they are, or how your life just couldn't possibly be complete without them. I don't even care that this statement costs me readers, listen to me carefully! Your pet is not your kid. See? That wasn't so hard.

For a lot of medical reasons, they wanted to induce Luke's birth, so Rachael and I slept in the hospital the night before the big day. Then, most of the next day we waited around for the action to happen. I was a little disappointed we didn't get to experience a Hollywood-style dash to the hospital, but honestly, that's overdone on screen and rarely true to life.

I won't give you the play-by-play of Luke's birth, but I will take a moment to repeat a piece of advice my father-in-law gave me as we were getting prepped to go back for the C-section. It was the same piece of advice my buddy John gave me a few weeks prior when his son was born. These experienced dads knew exactly what they were talking about. My father-in-law pulled me aside where Rachael wouldn't hear and said, "When you get in there, stay on your side of the drop cloth. You can't unsee that." For what it's worth, I followed that advice that day, but I failed to do so when my second son was born four years later. He was right. You can't unsee that. If your wife is going in for a C-section, *stay on your side of the drop cloth*.

One of the craziest parts of the actual birth itself was how many people were in the room for the big event. Not only did we have the normal delivery doctor and nurses, but we also had a team of people from the NICU (Neonatal Intensive Care Unit) ready to rush Luke to their part of the hospital. I don't know actual numbers, but it felt like 47 people crammed into one small room to witness the birth of our son. It was weird.

Okay, small side note here. As a preacher for over a decade now, I've been given the honor of officiating more weddings than I can remember. And while I understand those events hold tremendous significance for the people directly involved, for me, it tends to just be a Saturday that I'm working. With weddings and other special events, I understand how significant the day is, but unless I'm particularly close to the people, it's a job for me and a special day for them.

So, back to my son and the 47 people in attendance. To Rachael and me, it was a special day. To them, it was a Monday. Rachael and I were hanging on every moment, almost as if we had never done this before. They were catching up like they're standing around a water cooler instead of an operating table. "So, did you make it up to the lake this weekend?" "No, we had to go to the kid's soccer game and couldn't make it." "Say, did you guys get the invite to the movie?" "Oh, I don't know if I care to see that one. The last one we saw was awful." Again, it was weird.

Finally, at 6:06 pm on that Monday night it was baby time, and they lifted up our blue, slimy, beautiful baby boy. He weighed in at 5 lb. 10 oz. and measured 19 inches long. (I don't know why, but women always seem to want to know the measurements.) Rachael had just enough time to touch Luke once before they passed him off to the NICU team who immediately put him in a plastic box and rolled him to what would be his new home for the next month. He was breathing on his own, and we had a baby!

Little Luke's Big Heart

~

Back in 2007, when I was approaching graduation from ACU with my master's degree, I discovered a major scheduling problem on our calendar. On the same day I was to walk across a stage in Texas to get my piece of paper (they don't really even give you your piece of paper, they hand you a tube with an ad inside asking you to join their alumni group so that for the rest of your life they can solicit you for donations to your dear alma mater) my little sister was to walk across her stage in Oklahoma to get her undergrad degree. My parents were understandably torn because it's difficult to be in Oklahoma City, Oklahoma and Abilene, Texas at the same time. They talked about each of them attending a different graduation, leaving our family split right down the middle. But then I decided that instead of having our family divide, I would skip my graduation (much to my mother's dismay), travel to Oklahoma, and everyone could celebrate as one big happy family. My plan worked nicely, but if you've ever wanted to be in two different places at once, you can understand the dilemma.

In the moments after Luke's birth, I felt the same emotion of being torn, only much more so. I wanted to stay with my wife who'd just undergone major surgery, but I also wanted to go with my son who was in much more critical condition. Fortunately, Rachael and I had discussed it earlier, and the only decision that made sense was for me to go with Luke. All of Rachael's thoughts were with him anyway, and while her mom could stay with her, nobody except for me was allowed to go with Luke. And yet even though I knew it was the right decision, it still didn't feel right to leave my wife on an operating table and rush off with a team of doctors heading to the ICU. As Luke would teach me repeatedly as a parent, you often do what's critical and leave the important to someone else.

~

What's the best feeling in the world? Keep it clean please, this is a PG kind of book my mom will read. An ice-cold Coke on a hot day? Your first kiss? Your head hitting the cool pillow after a long day? Seeing your team win the big game? Crushing a major presentation? The typical person experiences several incredible highs, but the absolute best feeling of all is holding your baby for the very first time. Nothing compares. Absolutely nothing beats it. It's also instinctual. Telling a new parent, especially a new mom (again, it's not sexist if it's true), that she can't hold her baby is like holding a juicy cheeseburger (the best ones come from *Five Guys*; don't try passing off something from *In-N-Out* as the real thing) in front of a starving man and telling him he should just enjoy the smell. If you're holding onto the burger, you might lose a finger, and nobody would blame the man.

Rachael didn't get to hold Luke when he was first born. The OB held him next to her face for a moment, then they quickly rolled him away to NICU in a plastic box. I'm told most women experience so much comfort from holding their new baby that it takes much of the sting out of the physical trauma of childbirth. Rachael never got that. I'm also told it's incredibly comforting to the baby to experience skin to skin contact after every system in his body receives a shock by coming into the wide-open world. Luke never got that. The normal holding instinct of both mom and baby had to wait.

After Luke got to the NICU there were so many wires, tubes and stickers on him that holding him wasn't an option. We could reach into his plastic box and hold his hand or stroke his hair, but we did so with extreme caution, and we certainly couldn't lift him. Finally, a week after his birth, they put in a PICC line. I didn't know what a PICC line was at the time, but I would later learn that it's a more serious and stable version of a regular IV. That meant he was finally stable enough to be held. When the nurse turned to Rachael and asked, "How would you feel about holding him tonight for his feeding?" Rachael's gaze narrowed, she looked the lady straight in the eye, and in the most serious voice I've ever heard her use (which is saying something), she said, "Don't tease me." Holding your baby for the first time is serious business. Rachael sat down in the rocking chair with a pillow in her lap, and the nurse gently lifted Luke out of his plastic box and placed him into his mother's arms. I cried, Rachael *really* cried, and I could be wrong, but I'm pretty sure even the nurse cried.

Now here's the thing, with everything going on medically with Luke, he wasn't eating on his own. There was a feeding tube going down his throat through his nose, which they would pour milk down for about an hour. Since his digestive system wasn't up to full strength, they'd only pour in as much as he could absorb. It was always our prayer that he would absorb more so he could grow and get stronger. Also, Luke's lungs still weren't fully inflated, so he needed a significant amount of oxygen to keep his numbers on the monitor at an acceptable level. At the time he was working on two-thirds of one lung, and the other was completely collapsed. A couple of things happened for Luke when Rachael held him for an hour. First, he absorbed more milk during that feeding than he'd ever absorbed before, and second, the nurse needed to keep turning *down* his oxygen because his breathing improved so dramatically. After that feeding Luke slept as peacefully as we had ever seen. As much as Rachael enjoyed holding Luke, I'm pretty sure Luke liked it too.

Later that night when the doctor came to do her rounds, I mentioned to her how greatly Luke had improved when Rachael held him. She told me she'd seen this happen numerous times with babies in the NICU when they get held by their mama for the first time. I'm certainly glad plastic boxes for sick babies exist (Luke wouldn't have made it without his), but they're a poor, poor substitute for a mom. So, I return to my earlier question. What's the best feeling in the world? I have it on good authority from a woman who went to medical school, that it's a mother's touch.

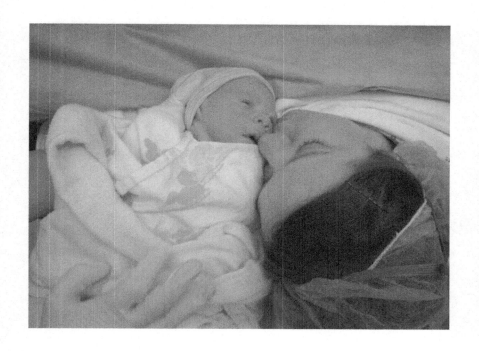

Luke's first kiss

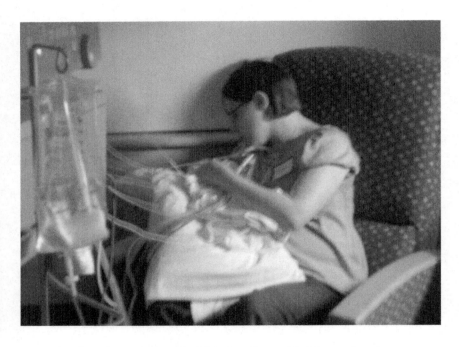

The first time Rachael held Luke. Sorry it's blurry, but the room was dark.

CHAPTER 5

Needing a Few Miracles

But for you who revere my name, the sun of righteousness will rise with healing in its rays.

Malachi 4:2a

I remember the Sunday night I preached my first real sermon. I was only a freshman in college, and I knew that what I wanted to do with my professional life was preach, but I was so terrified of public speaking that I didn't know if I could do it. I know that's kind of like a lifeguard who's afraid of swimming, but I knew if I got past my fear, I could have a meaningful career in pulpit ministry. Some people who've heard my preaching since then might have a different opinion, but hey, Bob Dylan somehow had a successful career in music, so what do people know? So, I spent an inordinate amount of time preparing my message, and the Saturday night before my debut, my nerves ensured that I slept about as well as a kid on Christmas Eve. All day Sunday the only thing I could think about was that maybe Jesus would come back any minute now, and if he did, then I wouldn't have to get up and preach in front of all those people.

In hindsight, my fear seems a little silly. That church was full of people who knew me, loved me, and would tell me what a great job I did even if I had passed out mid-homily. And, of course, public speaking is like just about anything else in life; after you do it enough times, you don't get nervous about it anymore. Today if you called me and told me I needed to preach right now, I wouldn't be nervous about it at all. I've actually had this happen to me once. I got a call from a wedding party that their preacher hadn't shown up. Thirty minutes later I preached a wedding. No big deal. With most fear, if you face it enough times, the fear wears off and loses its hold on you.

One arena which proves to be the exception to this rule is saying goodbye to your child as they go back to surgery. I don't care how many times you face it. It's hard every time. Also, I've never slept well the night before any of Luke's surgeries. All the hospitals we've been in let you stay with your child until the time they take them to the operating room. Then they let you walk with your child all the way to the doors of the OR where they pause for a minute to let mom and dad give their final hugs and kisses. Besides the hugs and kisses, Rachael tells Luke, "No funny business." Rachael and I always pray with him too. After this, your heart gets ripped out of your chest as they point you to the waiting room and wheel away your precious baby. It sucks every time, and you never get used to it.

Needing a Few Miracles

The first time Rachael and I experienced this was when Luke was four weeks old and went back for his first open-heart surgery. They gave us about a ninety percent chance of Luke surviving it. These are great odds, but still terrifying as you can't help but think about that ten percent who don't. We had a fantastic surgeon whom we loved dearly, and we filled the waiting room with family and friends. We were as ready as we could be.

The surgery itself proceeded according to plan. They worked on his heart, and it responded exactly as they wanted it to. I also appreciated the way the hospital did a good job of keeping us updated. They told us when the surgery started. They told us it was on schedule. And they told us when the surgery was completed. The problem came after they told us everything was finished and had gone well. When they took Luke up to his room, he crashed. I don't know exactly what crashing entails or what they did to stabilize him, but I know that if the heart-surgeon hadn't still been on the floor when he crashed, Luke wouldn't have survived. As it was, they were able to quickly put him on a machine called ECMO which basically does the job of your heart and lungs for you. (The next couple of sentences and the excerpt are tough, so feel free to skip to the next section if you're squeamish.) Because Luke was such a small baby at only four weeks old, the surgeon hadn't closed his chest cavity after the surgery. There was just a membrane placed over the hole. For a few days, a machine literally lived for Luke. The ECMO had one tube coming out of Luke's chest carrying oxygen-poor blood from his body to the machine which then put oxygen into his blood and carried it through another tube into the other side of Luke's chest.

Little Luke's Big Heart

An excerpt from Rachael's Facebook post on 6-8-2009:

We were told that one of the risks of ECMO is bleeding into the brain. They told us that if Luke began bleeding in his brain, they would have to take him off ECMO, and his heart would either have to work properly, or he would die. Before the surgery, Dr. Mendeloff told us that Luke would get much sicker after surgery before he got better. They told us when we saw him right afterward, we would see his chest still open (though covered with a skin-like membrane) to allow his heart room to swell, lots of new IV lines, he would look pale, and he would be cold to help his heart regulate his heartbeat. I thought I was prepared. I wasn't. When I walked into his room, the first thing I saw was his IV tree. Luke had two IV poles by his bed and I counted 18 different medications being given to him at the same time. When I looked at my son, he looked dead. I would have thought he was if I couldn't hear his heartbeat on the monitor. He was so pale and still. His body looked like he had been through a war. Like he had been chewed up and spit back out. He looked like a little doll chewed up by a dog and then sewn, taped, wired, and jerry-rigged back together. I was in shock. I couldn't speak, all I could do was cry. It didn't even look like my little Lucas.

~

Back before Luke's first surgery, when he was living in NICU, we took a lot of pictures. All new parents take a lot of pictures, and we will subject anyone to them whether you want to see our baby's pictures or not. We don't care. LOOK AT OUR BABY! He wasn't awake very often, so whenever he was, we would have a camera ready to capture the moment. After a short while, people are able to see past all the tubes and wires. We wanted more than anything in the world to be able to see our kid. We took a lot of pictures in NICU.

I have no pictures of Luke when he was on ECMO. Rachael and I never talked about it, but neither of us took pictures because he looked so unlike a person on that machine that we knew that no matter whether he lived or died, we didn't want to remember him that way. The surgeon told us that ECMO was hard on a baby's body and he would only be on it for a couple of days. After that, he would have to come off it. Then we would have to wait a day or two to see if he would survive. Sometimes babies make it; sometimes they just don't. I appreciated the surgeon kindly being straight with us and telling us what we were facing. The couple of days he was on ECMO will probably be the longest days of my life. When he came off of ECMO, we still had no idea how long our road home would be.

~

For many years I drove an old Nissan Sentra. It was a great car until about the last year I owned it. Towards the end, something would go wrong, the mechanic would fix it, and I'd think, "Okay, *now* I'm finally good to keep rolling." Unfortunately, it would only be a few weeks before something else would go wrong, and I'd start the cycle all over again. Finally, I cracked the head gasket, and the car drank coolant like people in the South drink sweet tea. It would cost more to fix the car than it was worth, so it was time for a new car.

That story resonate with anyone? When it's a car that keeps having different systems shut down, you eventually decide it's more trouble than it's worth, and you get a new one. When you watch your child's body do the same thing, it's one of the most demoralizing experiences you will ever face. For months on Luke's journey, it felt like every time we made headway somewhere, we'd take a new hit that made it feel like this would never end. We kept seeing the light at the end of the tunnel only to shortly thereafter find ourselves plunged back into darkness.

We got through the first heart surgery and through the ECMO nightmare. We thought after that we'd spend a couple of weeks in recovery, a few more weeks back in NICU, and then we'd go home to a relatively normal life. But the hits kept coming. Because Luke crashed so hard after his heart surgery, he went into kidney failure and needed dialysis while we waited to see whether his kidney function would return. They warned us that sometimes kids like Luke needed dialysis for the rest of their lives. All we could do was wait and see. What followed were some of the strangest prayers we've ever prayed asking God to please show us more pee! I've never been as happy to see pee in my entire life as when Luke started going on his own (TMI, but I don't care).

Then, as we were still dealing with his dialysis stuff, Luke's heart did something weird. I'm not sure if I fully understand what it was, but quite suddenly the top half of his heart was beating insanely fast (like over 200 bpm fast), and it wasn't in sync with the bottom half. This was a side effect from the surgery, and the doctors weren't entirely sure what to do about it. They tried treating it with medication for several days, but it wasn't working. They wanted to try him on a different medication, but his gut needed to absorb that medication. To top it all off, his gut wasn't working because his heart wasn't working. So, follow the logic, they really needed to fix his heart, so his heart would fix his gut, so his gut could absorb the medication that might fix his heart. Not good. They told us his heart could work like this for a while, but the insane pulse of his upper heart would eventually cause it to shut down. We, of course, wanted to know what kind of time-frame we were looking at, but they simply didn't know. Days? Maybe weeks? Who knows? Yet again, we tried to be mentally prepared to lose our baby.

Here's an excerpt from Rachael's Facebook post during this period, 7-10-2009:

The God we serve is able to do immeasurably more than we ask or even hope. He can heal Luke and make him whole. But we want the world to know that even if he does not, even if we lose our precious son, God is still worthy of worship and praise and honor. We acknowledge his love and power over all other gods.

One late night shortly after this, Rachael and I were exhausted, but we didn't want to go home. Instead, we just stared in dejection at the monitor and watched as his pulse numbers refused to come down. Then the coolest thing happened. One of our favorite doctors, Dr. Meyer, was working on the floor that night and came into our room. He called over the nurse (Kelly, one of our favorites) and said, "We're going to pray for this baby." It's not his job to pray for us. It's not the nurse's job to pray for us. But they knew some problems are bigger than a doctor's ability, and so they turned over Luke's heart to God. They laid hands on Luke and prayed. What we needed was a miracle. What we got next was an accident.

Little Luke's Big Heart

The very next day, they decided the best course of action would be to send a wire up into Luke's heart (heart catheterization) to see if there was anything physically wrong left over from the surgery to explain the rapid pulse. When the cardiologist did the procedure, they saw nothing illuminating, but they did have a small accident. The cardiologist wasn't supposed to touch anything while the wire was in Luke's heart, but he accidentally poked something in there. When he poked whatever it was, it changed Luke's heart rhythm.

About an hour later we were back in Luke's room and everyone—including two cardiologists, the intensivist and his nurse—was looking at a new pulse number. The next thing to do was to get a printout of exactly what his rhythm was doing. I'll never forget our beloved cardiologist, Dr. Kao, staring at the paper and saying, "This is good. We can shock him out of this rhythm." Wait. Did she say *shock*? They rolled in a crash cart, asked us to step outside, and then did the thing just like you see on TV where they say, "Clear!" and shock the patient. Only instead of it being on TV, it was real life, and instead of a random patient, it was our Luke. We literally stood in the hallway staring through the glass wall and watched them shock our baby back into a stable rhythm. Since then I've said that you really haven't lived until you've seen your kid shocked back into rhythm. I don't think I've ever been more awake than I was at that moment. It honestly wasn't nearly as dramatic as what you see on TV. All the medical professionals were calm and cool, and thanks to an accidental poke in his heart (inspired by prayer), the rhythm nightmare was finally over.

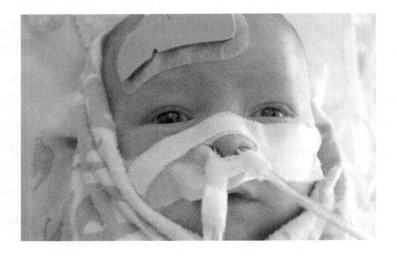

Luke from early hospital days

CHAPTER 6

A New Normal

Even youths grow tired and weary, and young men stumble and fall; but those who hope in the Lord will renew their strength.

Isaiah 40:30–31a

I appreciate a good cup of coffee. During our college/dating years, Rachael worked at Starbucks, so I spent a lot of time hanging around the coffee shop, doing homework, and making sure none of the other patrons flirted too hard with my girlfriend. The best side benefit of all was that I got free coffee! For most of our college years, every time I went to that Starbucks, whether she was on shift or not, everyone knew me as "Rachael's Boyfriend". By the time I got up to the bar, not only was my succulent beverage waiting for me, but I never needed to pay a dime. (I'm convinced that sitting next to the Gates of Heaven is a barista who can anticipate your order.) I died a little bit inside when she quit working there. I showed up for my coffee and the girl on the other side of the counter said, "That'll be $4.50, sir." My point is that I thought of myself as something of a coffee snob who knew good coffee from the stuff you buy in a jumbo tin at the grocery store. *I* only drank the good stuff.

When we started spending all our time at the hospital, I took a gamble on one of the free coffee machines they kept stationed all around the waiting areas. Seeing it there, I thought, "How bad can it be?" Turns out, it can be abhorrently bad. The flavor was appalling. The two positive things were that it was free, and it was hot. I couldn't even finish my first cup, and considering how much coffee I drink, that's saying something. Oddly enough, over the following weeks and months, something strange happened. *I began to like the bad coffee.* It's not that I stopped liking the good stuff (#starbuckssloverforever), and I'd still enjoy it whenever the opportunity arose, but I slowly got used to the waiting room sludge, and eventually, it just became normal coffee.

I told you that story because Rachael and I spent about a year of our lives going to the hospital every day. At first, everything about it felt wrong, was uncomfortable, and I wanted to be anywhere else but there, but over the weeks and then months, hospital life became normal life. For the longest time, Rachael and I repeated our mantra to each other, "This is what we do."

Our routine was set. During the week Rachael would get up and go straight to the hospital (about a 45-minute drive) while I went into the office to work. Then sometime after lunch, I'd head to the hospital as well.

A New Normal

We'd normally take turns going to eat dinner, and then after the evening shift-change, we'd head home. Usually, we'd watch TV together for about thirty minutes before going to bed (which I felt guilty about because we could have spent thirty minutes longer at the hospital), then we would get up early and do it all over again. On the weekends we spent all day Saturday at the hospital as a family. Sunday morning was church, after which we would go to the hospital in two cars because I needed to preach the Sunday night sermon. A few of those sermons, especially the evening ones, were no doubt terrible. Memories of that time leave me feeling exhausted, but we did it because we simply wanted to be with our son. Hospital life became normal life.

~

As a preacher, I can't resist a nice, numbered list. So, here's my advice to you if you are facing a long (anything more than two or three days) stay in the hospital with your loved one.

1. Make the nurses your best friends.

You will interact with the nurses much more than the doctor or anybody else during your hospital stay, so it pays to get to know them and be friends with them. They will be your best teachers if you let them. We formed such good relationships with some of our nurses that three of them drove all the way out to Terrell to attend Luke's first birthday party. We still keep up with some of those ladies who have loved Luke from his earliest days. I really can't say enough good things about nurses.

While the vast majority of the nurses we met through our journey were awesome, we ran into a couple we didn't like. If you get a nurse with which you don't feel comfortable, don't hesitate to tell the charge nurse and request that you not get that nurse again. If I remember correctly, we only did that once in all the time we spent at the hospital. Just remember that the hospital exists to provide a service for you, so you have more say-so than you may think.

2. Learn as much as you can about what's going on.

Hospital life can be overwhelming. It seems like there are a million machines, wires and tubes even if you're just in for something simple. The faster you know what all the equipment does, the better you'll feel about what's going on. A lot of it is just there to monitor stuff and isn't as scary as it looks. Ask your nurse to explain what the numbers on the screen mean. Ask what medications they're giving your kid. When the therapist comes in to give your child a breathing treatment or to exercise something, ask questions. Most people like to talk about their jobs, and medical people are no exception. Also, don't be afraid to say you don't understand something. Medical jargon is its own language. When hospital people start throwing around stuff like "we give it BID" or "he's NPO" everyone knows exactly what those abbreviations mean except for you, so you should find out. You'll feel better, and they're happy to explain it to you.

Later in our journey, when we were at Disney World for our Make a Wish trip, we needed to take Luke into the ER. When we got to the hospital, I was describing everything going on with Luke using the medical jargon I knew, because it really was the fastest way to talk. As soon as there was a lull in the action one tech turned to me and asked, "So what do you do in the medical field?" Me? What I do in the medical field is take care of my kid.

Another good example is when I found a new piece of equipment in Luke's hospital room. It was a small device that delivered an electric shock, so the doctor could determine how snowed under Luke was on his medicine. Well, I wanted to see just how shocking this thing was; I mean, they use it on little kids, how painful could it be? (Don't get ahead of me.) What I didn't know was the machine had multiple settings, so when I put the stupid thing next to my forearm, I gave myself a MUCH larger jolt than I intended. Moral of the story: Don't play with stuff that's not for you. My second moral of the story is don't tell the nurses what you did because they will tell each other and make fun of you for weeks.

3. Don't feel guilty about taking a minute for yourself or your marriage.

At the prompting of Rachael, I will include an entire section about self-care later, but keep in mind that you shouldn't feel guilty about taking a minute away when you need it. I mentioned earlier how I felt guilty for watching a sitcom at the end of the night before bed, but in good 20–20 hindsight I now know better. My sitting in the hospital for an extra thirty minutes a night wasn't going to help anything, and decompression at the end of the day was necessary for my mental health. I'm not saying you should schedule a golf trip with your buddies, but take a few minutes to watch an episode of *The Office* or something. It will really help in the long run.

On the other hand, we observed several babies in the hospital who were absolutely, straight up neglected. When we spent five weeks in our second hospital learning how to use all of Luke's home medical equipment, we shared a room with a little girl whose mom rarely came by. When she did, she didn't stay long and spent more time talking on her cell phone than talking to her baby. I'm guessing if you're reading this book that's not you, but I really felt sorry for those poor kids whose parents weren't there.

4. Forget about work.

I don't have exact numbers, but in the first year of Luke's life, during which he had two open-heart surgeries, multiple "minor" surgeries, and we almost lost him more than once, I preached about eighty sermons. That's *insane*. It also doesn't include the two classes a week I was teaching. Okay, that's not only insane, it's beyond stupid. And I know why I did it; I was a young, insecure preacher, things were not perfect at the church, and I used work to help keep my mind busy. But just because I understand the why of it, doesn't mean it was a good idea. If you have the ability to take real time off (and I understand not everyone can), then focus on your family and have faith that you're not so important work can't live without you for a while.

5. Ask for stuff.

People want to help, so let them. Don't be afraid to ask a friend to cut your yard or bring you food. There's no reason for you to be prideful and self-reliant. Let your friends help! Try to think of a few things you would like help with. When friends say they want to help, but don't know how, they usually mean it.

6. If you know your hospital stay is coming, learn the eating places in and around the hospital ahead of time.

Learn which places have carry-out and learn the hours of the eating places in the hospital. You may think, "The hospital has a cafeteria, I'll eat there!" But hospital food is expensive, and you'll tire of it quicker than you think.

7. Use the hospital social worker.

This person is great for helping you navigate insurance companies and find cheap hotels. The social worker is also the best person to ask for any information you might need that's not medically related.

8. Know that weekends slow way down.

If your loved one really needs a procedure or surgery done on the weekend, then the hospital will get it done. But typically, in hospital world, if it can wait until Monday, it will wait until Monday.

9. Know that your first few days are some of the hardest, but once you get into a rhythm and things start to become routine, it gets a little easier.

The faces coming into your room start to look familiar, the beeps and alarms start to make sense, and your brain starts to relax. You can do this!

~

I saw part of a *Mythbusters* episode once in which they experimented with Chinese water torture (which turns out to be about as Chinese as a fortune cookie). If you're not familiar with this particular form of torture, it involves immobilizing a victim and then repeatedly hitting the exact same spot on their forehead with a drop of water over an extended period of time. The idea is that if you do this long enough, you can drive a person insane. It's not that any single drop of water is all that irritating or harmful, but the small irritant repeated to what feels like infinity slowly builds up in your body until you snap. On *Mythbusters*, they strapped down Cute

Girl (I think that's her name), and after an hour and a half of dripping, she couldn't take it anymore, and they let her up. Myth confirmed; water torture works.

When you spend an extended amount of time in the hospital, the small irritant that never leaves you alone and threatens your sanity is the beeping. Every single machine in a hospital beeps. The IV beeps. The ventilator beeps. The BP cuff beeps. If you need a nurse, you press a button, and guess what it does? The worst beeping in our experience, however, was the pulse oximeter monitor. If you don't know what one is, it's the little red light they stick on your finger (or elsewhere if you're a baby) whenever you're in the hospital to measures the amount of oxygen in your blood. A normal adult has an oxygen concentration reading a couple of points shy of a hundred percent. Luke lived for a long time in the high sixties and low seventies, and that was while he was getting extra oxygen. For a lot of Luke's life, the number that has determined whether he was doing well or not was his pulse ox number. Whenever the number went too low, the machine started beeping. Years later, I can remember *exactly* what it sounded like.

Have you ever watched a sport on TV and thought maybe through sheer force of will you could change what's happening on the screen? Like you're watching a football game, and you're willing your running back to get a few more yards so he can find the end zone? In your rational mind, you know that staring at a screen will change absolutely nothing. You could miss the entire game, check the score tomorrow, and it will be the same whether or not you applied your will to it. You know that, but if someone came into your living room mid-game while you're shouting at the screen and said, "Why don't we just turn this off, so you can relax," not only would you *not* be more relaxed, but you'd likely hurt someone.

Okay, I can't tell you how many hours Rachael and I spent staring at a pulse ox monitor trying to get Luke's numbers to go up just through the force of our will. *If he can just climb a few points higher, it'll stop the beeping! Come on Luke, you can do it!* There were a few instances in which the nurses tried to angle the monitor so we didn't see it anymore and said things like, "You don't need to worry about this. I'll keep an eye on it, so you don't have to." While I appreciated what they were trying to do, if I didn't see numbers that let me know how my son was doing, then I was not more relaxed, I was just mad at them—and more stressed—for taking my numbers away. If the Gates of Heaven feature a barista with free coffee, I'm fairly sure the Gates of Hell torture you with beeping.

~

Have you ever had one of those times in your life when it seems like all the planets align, the coffee kicks in, the world slows down, and an idea hits your brain with such clarity that you know you see something *exactly* as it is? Have you ever had a thought you knew would stick with you forever? Maybe it was the moment you realized you would spend the rest of your life with someone. Maybe it was a God-given moment when you knew you needed to change your life. Maybe it was a time you were staring across the ocean, or out from the top of a mountain, and you found clarity. Most of us live life at such a speed that whenever we finally do slow down and catch such a moment, it hits us upside the head like a two by four because it happens so rarely. We should treasure those moments.

I don't remember the exact specifics of when on our journey it happened. It would have been during one of Luke's earlier hospital stays, but I can remember exactly where I was standing in Medical City Hospital when such a moment of startling clarity hit. I had left Luke's hospital room to go eat, and while I was out, I paused for a few moments to stare at the large TV in the expansive lobby. I can't even tell you what compelled me to stop, but on the TV were these two sports commentators, dressed in expensive suits (probably in a garish color of blue, or with awkward pinstripes since those guys always dress like they didn't get enough attention when they were kids). With deadly serious expressions on their faces, they were arguing about who they thought would win the upcoming Super Bowl.

Now, I have a healthy appreciation for watching football (Boomer Sooner! Also, if DeMarco Murray is healthy in 08' they beat the Tebow-led Florida Gators for that natty, no doubt, no doubt in my mind.), but I was on my way back up to sit next to my son, who was being kept alive by nothing more than tubes, machines and the grace of God. So, while I'm thinking about literal life or death issues, these guys are arguing about who will win a game played by adults who have spent their entire lives playing a game that *doesn't matter!* Two grown men cared so much about a game that would be forgotten as soon as the next season of NFL action started that they were arguing over it.

Unless you're a football nut or your team won it all that year, nobody cares who won a game sometime last decade. And even if you are a football nut, it still doesn't matter. None of the entertainment we consume (and consumes us) throughout our lives matters. It doesn't matter who got voted off the island. It doesn't matter who gets to dance with what star next week. It doesn't matter what Simon Cowell said after an amazing performance. It doesn't matter how many likes, up-votes, re-tweets or comments your clever/sexy/funny/sad story got. It doesn't matter when the next Star Wars or Marvel movie is coming out. It doesn't matter that you shattered the record at your last track meet, or got a standing ovation at your recital, or crushed your latest business proposal. It doesn't matter. Let me say that again. It. Doesn't. Matter.

So many of the things we care about desperately just flat out don't matter. Rachael and I spent a lot of time in ICU rooms with Luke. Never once did I witness a couple arguing over the TV remote. Never once did I hear anyone bicker about getting a new car or wearing popular clothes. I won't speak for anyone else, but I need to repent for all the time, emotional energy, and mental capacity I've wasted on stuff that really does not matter at all.

I had an older professor once at ACU who said he regularly ran into people who weren't ready for the next step of spiritual maturity because they were still in the season of life in which they were "filling buckets." What he meant is that much of our lives are consumed by growing our bank accounts bigger, climbing the corporate ladder higher, or achieving whatever life goals we've set up for ourselves. Unfortunately, by chasing after all the things we think will bring meaning to our lives we end up filling a bunch of buckets but leaving all the stuff that actually matters unattended. The world defines success in one way, yet it is so broken.

Don't buy into the broken definitions offered by the world, or you'll find yourself screaming at a football team on TV while missing the life God calls you to lead.

~

A couple of years ago I sent my sister a packet with instructions for what to do in case something tragic happens to my wife and me. Inside are all the details for our insurance policies, our bank information, our will, our instructions for how to take care of the kids and so forth. I did all of this because on my afternoon commutes I sometimes catch *The Dave Ramsey Show*. Dave told me to put a death-packet together for my children, so, like a good second-born child, I dutifully followed his instructions. Now, if I should die in a massive fireball because instead of watching the road I was busy arguing with Rachael over her (lack of) navigating abilities, I can roast in confidence, because my final instructions are in place. Sorry, that was a little darker than I intended it, but we'll just roll with it. Anyway, as an adult, it's important to have your affairs reasonably in order, because if the worst should happen, you want to be ready. It's morbid. We don't like to think about it, and hopefully, we never need it, but we want to be responsible, so we plan for the worst-case scenarios.

While it's normal to plan for worst-case scenarios for yourself or even your parents, it's abnormal to have to plan out worst-case scenarios for your child. After Luke's birth, we knew things could go either way. While we were hopeful, we also guarded ourselves as much as we could against the possible pain that would come if he didn't make it. Before he even made it to his first surgery, he was struggling in NICU to simply breathe, and one of the doctors pulled Rachael aside to have what has to be an incredibly difficult conversation for a doctor to initiate. The neonatologist wanted us to know that the hospital would support whatever final decision we as Luke's parents wanted to make. We, of course, were given the option of pursuing every medical treatment available, but if it looked like things weren't trending in the right direction, one of the choices was to take Luke home and let him die peacefully without all the tubes, IVs, surgeries and other extraordinary measures. The doctor needed us to know that the medical staff would not judge us if we decided that enough was enough for Luke, and it was time to stop. As odd as it sounds, I really appreciated the doctor taking the time to explain that to us.

A few months later, I got a call from a company that specializes in creating final memories of kids who didn't make it. They photoshop out all the tubes and wires from pictures and make handprints and footprints. I'm not sure what else they do, but the girl on the other end of the line spoke with tenderness and compassion. That's a hard job, and I'm glad companies like that and girls like her exist, but I wish the need didn't. I was thankful at the time to tell them we didn't require their services, but I held on to her contact information, you know, just in case.

I also had an interesting experience a few months later regarding the local funeral home in Terrell. Our church had several connections to the funeral home, and we also had an older congregation, so I worked with the funeral directors regularly. They were good people, and we knew each other by name. (FYI, if a preacher ever calls you "Brother," or "Sister," or an older lady "Sweetie," it means he's totally forgotten your name. I end up calling a lot of people these family names.) One day when there was a funeral service in our church building, the funeral director, through my associate minister because it's too awkward to do it directly, told me that if we needed them, they would facilitate Luke's service for free. It was a really nice gesture. Again, because it was too awkward, I never thanked them for it.

On a few different occasions, Rachael and I talked through some things we wanted for the worst-case scenario arrangements. We had already decided who would preach the service. Being the preacher makes that a more complicated question. An accountant can do his own taxes, but it would have been impossible for me to do my own son's service. We also knew we likely wouldn't stay in Texas forever, so we planned for his final resting place to be back in Oklahoma where we still had family. Some conversations are hard but necessary.

I'm sorry this section is a bit morbid, but I feel it's important for you to know that when a family goes through something like what we went through with Luke, the worst-case scenario is always on their mind. At least for us, the feeling stayed for a long time. A piece of it may stay forever. The only thing that makes the feeling bearable is our faith that God will ultimately win the victory even if we suffer through that worst-case scenario. I know that God knows what it's like to see his son die. Because of that, I can trust him to take care of my son, even if the worst should happen.

Our family as we neared the end of our first hospital stay

CHAPTER 7

Self–Care Isn't Selfish

Remember the Sabbath day by keeping it holy.

Exodus 20:8

Anytime I watch old television shows or movies one thing that most shocks my modern sensibilities is the prevalence of smoking. Turn on *I Love Lucy,* and chances are she's puffing away. *Breakfast at Tiffany's* features Audrey Hepburn with her iconic, chic, cigarette holder. Even a show like *Mad Men,* set in the 60s, depicts normal life as a series of smoke-filled rooms and conversations. Of course, back in my grandparents' day, smoking was a normal thing.

Everyone did it, and nobody thought it was as deadly as we now know it to be. Smoking was just the way things were. [1]

I believe that when my grandchildren look back on my day, the thing that will shock their modern sensibilities and cause them to shake their heads in wonderment is the busyness (pace, stress, and pressures) we live with today. Our busyness is a normal thing, everyone does it, and we don't pay attention to how deadly we already know it to be. Busyness is just the way things are.

Maybe your story is different, but in my own conversations with people, I will often ask them how they're doing, and instead of telling me anything about the blessings or stresses of their lives, they will respond by telling me how busy they are. "Oh Preacher, I've been running like crazy. I'm so busy." And then I immediately feel this irrational pressure to compare my busyness to theirs in an effort to prove that, no, they think they're busy? I'm the one who's busy! I do this as if there's some imaginary prize awarded to the person who most overfilled their calendar. It's insane, but I believe the main reason we play this game is that many of us derive our self-worth based on all the wrong stuff. We all too often define who we are by our accomplishments rather than on our place as loved children of God. We wrongly value *doing* over *being*.

---

[1] This story has nothing to do with this book, but it's too good not to tell. Once when I was watching *Mad Men* on Netflix, I came into work the next day and complained to my office admin that on *Mad Men* when Mr. Draper enters his office, his secretary immediately jumps up, takes his coat, and gets him his coffee. Why didn't I get that kind of treatment? Without missing a beat, she looked at me and said, "Well if *you* looked like Don Draper, I'd get you your coffee." Ouch.

Self-Care Isn't Selfish

God knew this was going to be a struggle for us. The longest of the Ten Commandments is actually commandment number four in which he mandated a day of rest for his people. God specifically wanted his people to find their self-worth in their relationship to him instead of in how busily they could accomplish a bunch of stuff. This lesson is hard for us, as most of us think that the stuff we're doing is so important that we can't afford to slow down. Surely the world will quit turning if I don't get through my agenda, right? But remember, Jesus knew how to take the Sabbath, and I don't care how important you think you are, you're not nearly as important *as the Son of God.* Fair enough?

My reason for bringing this up is that sitting in a hospital room forced me to lay aside my busyness, re-prioritize my life, and for a while, just *be.* Now, I'm an introvert by nature, so I like to think I'm better at silence than most, but I believe long stretches in the hospital could try the patience of even the most seasoned monk. Most of us aren't used to silence, we wake up to a radio or TV, play music in the car, and basically use our technology to banish any silence that might creep into our day. My appeal to you though is if you are facing a lengthy hospital stay, allow that forced Sabbath to remind you of why God commanded a Sabbath in the first place. When we get to a place in which we have no control, it forces us to rely on the only one who has ever really been in control. When we finally learn how to let go, we can start to see how foolish it was to sacrifice our lives to the idol of busyness.

Little Luke's Big Heart

~

I don't know if I ever did self-care well while we were in the hospital, so this section is kind of like me giving you advice on buying a used car. Just because I did it once, doesn't mean I know what I'm doing. Now that I've completely undercut my credibility, here's my list of stuff to do to take care of yourself while your loved one is in the hospital.

1. Take walks.

Your body is not made to sit still. It would be great for you to take a thirty-minute break several times a day and explore the hospital. I'm now *really* familiar with the layouts of some hospitals in Dallas. I could no doubt quote an impressive medical study here to back up my walking point, but you don't need it because we all know it's true.

2. Get sleep.

Everyone knows hospitals are supposed to be the place where people go to get better, but ironically, they are the hardest place in which to get actual rest. I can't tell you how many times Luke would finally get into a deep sleep only to have the x-ray tech insist that now is the time to shine a bright light in his face and lift him onto a board. Now, there isn't too much you can do to change the resting situation in the hospital room, but whenever you have time to go home or back to the hotel for a bit, your number one priority needs to be sleep. Everything is worse when you're sleep deprived, and everything works better when you've gotten some good sleep. If you need to ask someone else to go to the hospital for a while and sit with your kid, do it.

3. Drink water.

Self-Care Isn't Selfish

Can I be honest with you for a second? This one is only on the list because Rachael told me to put it on here. She's probably right that you should drink water, but in the interest of not being a total hypocrite, I feel the need to let you know I almost never drank water, and instead consumed boatloads of coffee and Coke. At any rate, stay well hydrated. It helps.

4. Connect with friends.

Hospitals can be lonely and isolating. One of my favorite memories of our time in the hospital was a day when our group of couple friends all showed up with a stack of pizzas and we spent about an hour having a pizza party in a side hallway of the hospital. I don't know what this will look like for you, but do what you can to connect with your friends.

Remember that unless you take care of yourself, you won't be able to take care of your loved one. It's like when you're on a plane and they tell you to put on your own oxygen mask before assisting your kid. It's not selfish to take time to do the things on this list, it's common sense. The problem is sometimes we think when our loved one is sick that the rules no longer apply to us, and we try to muscle through by sheer force of will. Don't be that person!

~

The other day I read through the Sermon on the Mount (Matthew 5–7), which is a large collection of things Jesus taught in his ministry, and I have a couple of objections I'd like to make. For the most part, interpreting what Jesus says isn't all that difficult. The struggle comes in actually doing what he says. I struggle with doing some of the things (okay, *most* of the things)

Jesus says in this teaching, but the teaching I object to the most is his instructions on worry. It all starts in 6:11, during the Lord's Prayer, when Jesus models for us a prayer in which he says, "Give us today our daily bread." Really Jesus? I object. I don't want daily bread, I want six months to a year's worth of bread. I want to know that I have everything I need for a long time down the road. I'm not really cool with this idea of having just enough light for the step I'm on. God, how am I supposed to be okay with you just taking care of me for today, when I don't know how you will get me through tomorrow? Walking by faith is all well and good, but Lord, if it wouldn't be too much trouble, I would prefer to walk by sight.

Then starting in 6:25 Jesus has a whole section on how we should be more like birds and flowers who don't worry about anything. Again, Jesus, I object. My life is infinitely more complicated than any flower. I have a mortgage, I gotta go to work every day, my kids demand *lots* of attention, and there's always something going on at church that could be better. So Lord, how am I expected to take care of all my important business if I don't worry about it? Now, of course, Jesus is right. I should have greater faith, because after all, when has worrying ever helped anything? I can't tell you how many hours I wasted worrying over things that might happen to Luke. Some of them did, and some of them didn't, but worrying certainly never changed any of them.

Besides worrying about the systems of his body, like his cardiovascular or pulmonary systems, I worried a great deal about his development. For a while, we worried that he would be deaf. Then we worried that he would not speak, or walk, or eat. These were not unreasonable concerns since doctors and therapists were warning us they were real possibilities. So, I worried. And then I worried some more. Then ironically, I spent time worrying that I was worrying too much. Of course, now he's only deaf when he doesn't want to hear what Mom and I are saying, we can't get him to shut up (or quit singing the same song on repeat), and he gets around just fine. Maybe I should take a lesson from the birds and flowers after all.

~

Recently, my youngest son, Sam, has started to understand the value and importance of money. We regularly tell him he can't have something he wants because "Well, son, that toy/activity costs money, and you don't have any." And I could totally afford to buy the Power Ranger or a trip to the bowling alley, but I just refuse to be that parent that lets their kids set the agenda and get everything they want. Then Sam got smarter and started asking, "How do you get money?" Rachael immediately put him to work. For about an hour's worth of chores, he earns one shiny quarter. Finally, he earned three dollars in quarters. The next time he asked to rent a movie on Amazon, he met my "You don't have any money" line with "Wanna bet? Check out the contents of my Batman piggy bank!" To most of us, a quarter isn't a big deal. If we saw one on the street, we might not even pick it up. But from Sam's perspective, it's big money. I would never look down on my son for thinking a quarter is a big deal because I know that at his age he simply can't possess the perspective necessary to imagine something the size of a house payment. Big money is all a matter of perspective.

Perspective matters! I want to end this chapter with a final lesson that's bitten me more than once. If you ever become a hospital veteran, be careful about dismissing others who don't have your medical perspective.

You likely have figured out by now that I work at a church, and one of the things from which I derive a certain amount of amusement is the variety of ways people make prayer requests for themselves and their family members. At one extreme, I encounter people who think every time they get a hangnail or a headache they need us to send out an emergency email updating the congregation on their condition. (I'm exaggerating here, but only slightly.) Then at the other extreme, I'll find out someone was in the hospital getting a major organ transplant, and they didn't tell us because "Oh, well, I didn't want to bother anybody."

Because of all our experiences with Luke, Rachael and my perspectives on what constitutes a serious medical issue are a bit out of whack with that of the general population. I'm of the opinion that if it doesn't require a weeklong stay in ICU, you should just walk it off. Once Luke was getting ready to go in for a heart catheterization (where they run a line into your heart) so they could put in a patch. I felt like that was worthy of prayer, but when people asked what we were going in for, I said, "Oh it's just a heart cath. We'll likely only be in ICU for a night at most. It's no big deal." One of our new members almost fell to the floor and said, "I can't imagine what all you've gone through if you can call *that* no big deal." Like I said, my perspective is skewed.

Now, where this skewed perspective has gotten me in trouble is when I need to minister to church members dealing with health struggles. Nobody likes the jaded preacher coming in and telling them to just shake it off. I've never *actually* done that, but I've been tempted. It turns out that mercy and kindness might not be my strongest spiritual gifts. I have to remind myself that even though I don't think someone's sickness is that big of a deal, for them, it's huge. There's no such thing as "minor" surgery when it's your surgery. We will have an entire chapter devoted to comparisons later on but remember that in the same way I'd never dismiss my son's financial concerns, we need to minister to others from their perspective, not our own.

CHAPTER 8

There's No Place Like Home

Lord, hear my voice. Let your ears be attentive to my cry for mercy.

Psalm 130:2

I had a serious theological argument with a "friend" once about whether or not *Napoleon Dynamite* was a good movie. I defended the theologically *correct* position that the movie is hilarious. The scene where the old farmer shoots the cow in front of the bus full of kids? That's worth the price of the movie by itself. My wife and I still occasionally yell at each other, "Your mom goes to college!" and it's funny every time. My "friend" argued that it's the dumbest movie he'd ever seen. (That's why I now type "friend" in quotes. Can you honestly be friends with someone who has such a lack of taste?) Okay, in all seriousness, I can understand why some people thought it was a good movie, and some people hated it. *Napoleon* is only for those of us with a highly refined sense of the comedic. I have certainly seen movies before that other people thought were great, but I thought were horrible. I may lose my Georgia residency for this, but I couldn't even make it all the way through *Gone with the Wind*. Seriously, Scarlett whines through the *entire* movie. Some movies are clearly better than others, and I understand that people will have their own tastes. But beyond doubt, one of the worst movies ever created in the history of humanity has to be an educational film Rachael and I saw about caring for a child with a tracheostomy.

For this part of the story, you will need a little background information. After Luke recovered from his first heart surgery, we began exploring what it would take to get him home from the hospital. We discovered several things. I'm sure there are exceptions to this, but this was our experience. You can't go home intubated. (Intubated is when a tube goes in your mouth and down your throat and connects to the machine that breathes for you.) You also can't go home unless you have a reliable means of getting nutrition. You either have to eat or have a feeding tube going in somewhere. Also related to the eating thing, it's necessary to have a means of receiving medication. This can be in the form of either an IV port or oral meds that can go through the feeding tube. Breathing happens before eating and meds, so our first step was getting extubated.

There's No Place Like Home

So, the day finally came when they decided Luke was breathing well enough that they would try taking the tube out of his throat. Rachael and I watched from the hallway as they took it out, then immediately had to put it back in. The doctor told us he just wasn't ready yet, but we shouldn't lose heart because they would try again when he grew stronger. They tried again several days later, and again the attempt immediately failed. They told us they would try one more time in two weeks, but if it failed again, they would have to take more drastic measures. Drastic measures meant surgically installing a tracheostomy, or "trach" for short. This meant they would cut a hole in his throat just below his vocal cords then put a tube into it which would allow him to breathe and use a portable ventilator. They would also put another hole in his stomach, then put in another tube (it's called a g-button) through which we could give him food and medicine.

We wanted our baby home, but the last thing we wanted was to take him home with a boatload of medical equipment and have him connected to a bunch of tubes. To prepare for potentially leaving the hospital with a trach, the doctor sent us home with an educational DVD about life with a tracheostomy child. Okay, I do metaphors for a living, and I've got nothing in the way of a metaphor for describing to you how terrible this video was. The mom in the video never once smiled. You could tell she was in pain the entire time. The kid in the video was maybe two, and even though there were multiple scenes of him playing with toys and on swings, he never looked in any way like a normal kid doing normal things. The video contained a little decent information, but it made having a kid with a trach look like a family with a prison sentence. I still remember how we felt as we sat on our brown microfiber couch in the living room watching that video and thinking "Please God, don't let us have to do that."

Our next step was to do the only thing we knew to do; we prayed. God had overcome bigger odds than this in Luke's life. He could easily fix Luke's airway and make it possible for us to go home tube-free. I'm a big believer in praying for specific things, so we prayed for exactly what we wanted God to do. I'm also a big believer in asking the family of God to pray for specific things, so we mobilized our prayer warriors. Rachael wrote an impassioned plea on social media, and I copied it. Literally, hundreds of people prayed specifically that in two weeks' time when they pulled out Luke's breathing tube, he would be able to breathe without assistance.

The stories we like to tell in church are those in which God responds powerfully. We prayed Luke would make it to term. God answered powerfully, proving the doctors wrong! We prayed for Luke when he almost died after his first surgery, and God answered with the gift of life. As a preacher, I love to tell stories like that because they inspire people to lean into God, and they help invigorate people to pray! Not as fun to tell are the stories in which we offered up hundreds of prayers, and instead of witnessing God's might, we saw nothing. We prayed our hearts out that we wouldn't have to go down the road of getting a trach, but we went down that road anyway. God chose not to answer our prayers. After the two weeks were up, a surgeon put two more holes in our baby, and we learned what it would look like to go home with a tracheostomy/feeding tube kid.

There's No Place Like Home

~

A phrase I've often heard used incorrectly in Christian circles is "the dark night of the soul". This phrase appears as the title of a work written by the 16th-century Spanish mystic, St. John of the Cross. Contrary to pop-level usage, he didn't mean "I'm going through a really hard time right now." Instead, he was referring to (according to my extremely amateurish understanding—you'll have to forgive me, that dude's hard to read) a season encountered by many monastics in which it feels like all they're getting from God is absence. Instead of experiencing God's presence in your life when you pray, you get empty silence. This is obviously disconcerting, but St. John encouraged his readers that this was actually a time in which Christians could deepen their faith and learn to have an even greater reliance on God.

The "dark night" language is overused, and I won't fully apply it to our situation here (I'm not a very good mystic), but as a Christian who tries to rely on prayer, I couldn't help but think of St. John of the Cross as our prayers were met with silence. What do you do when you, and hundreds of other people, pray in faith for a specific, good, unselfish outcome, and instead of getting the healing you asked for, you get a trial? I can't fully answer that question. I can say that even though we didn't get the answer we wanted, we did get the strength we needed to endure our trial, and in the final analysis, God showed us his strength was enough. Because God continued to give us the strength we needed for each step of our journey, I can honestly say our faith was deepened. Again, I'm not saying that's why God didn't answer our prayers the way we wanted, but I am saying that if you're in a season in which God seems to be absent, stick with God, keep moving forward, and remember that night eventually gives way to dawn.

~

When I was a kid, I couldn't wait to be an adult. No more sisters pestering me. (The struggle was real.) No more draconian, mandated bedtimes by totalitarian parents. (I was a fun kid.) As an adult, I could go where I wanted, when I wanted, dress how I wanted, stay as long as I wanted, and nobody would tell me differently. (All you married guys just chuckled mournfully as you read that last line.) Little did I know that becoming an adult meant learning a whole new set of skills and information I would need to successfully navigate the world. Suddenly, I needed to learn about car insurance, taxes, lawn-care, laundry, budgeting, scheduling, and a whole host of other things they don't teach you in school (oddly enough, trigonometry never came up again after the eleventh grade). It turns out that moving from one stage of life to another requires you to gain a new level of competencies just to keep your head above water.

Moving from "married couple" to "married couple with a baby" is a similar life stage move. Suddenly a whole new list of competencies comes along that you really can't prepare for until you're in the thick of it. A new parent must learn how to feed a baby, wash a baby, clothe a baby, pack a bag for a baby, pack a car for a baby, play with a baby, and basically reorient all of life to include a baby. You remember sleeping through the night? Not anymore! It's a fairly steep learning curve, but most of us have our parents, older siblings, or other friends who can help out, or at the very least offer wise counsel (in addition to all the unsolicited advice). In the normal course of events, you start out completely overwhelmed, terrified, and a little naïve, but you finally settle down into a nice rhythm of life just in time for the next life stage to shake things up one more time (enter the dreaded toddler).

With Luke, Rachael and I experienced this same baby life stage learning curve, only on steroids. Not only that, but we couldn't turn to our parents or friends for advice on how to navigate it. A few months after Luke's birth the doctors deemed him healthy enough to go home for a few months before it would be time for a return trip for his second open-heart surgery. But before we got to go home, we needed to go to a special facility for an open-ended amount of time (it ended up being five weeks) while Rachael and I learned how to take care of a special needs baby in our own home. As we found out, there was a lot to learn.

We were required to learn how to work a ventilator—which is nothing more than a ridiculously expensive box that breathed for Luke. We, in reality, took home two ventilators (just in case, because, you know, BREATHING). And because Luke had a tracheostomy, we needed to learn how to care for the trach as well. There's nothing quite as nerve-wracking as changing a trach on a baby. You know he can't breathe until you get it in, so, please, don't screw up. We learned how to work a feeding pump which transferred milk/formula and medication from a bag, through a tube, and into the surgically implanted button in Luke's stomach. Luke was also constantly connected to a heart monitor which measured his oxygen levels and pulse. He needed oxygen tanks to breathe, a long list of medications for a long list of reasons, and a suction machine as a constant companion because that went with the trach. He was a complicated kid.

We took weeks to learn all of this, but we worked hard at it because we loved our son. More than anything else right then we just wanted him home. Somebody famous once said, "There's no place like home." She was right.

~

I read a story on the internet the other day (so you know it must be true) of a man in Eastern Europe who had somehow fallen through the cracks in the governmental bureaucracy. After a period of years, the government declared him officially dead. The only problem was that he wasn't dead, so when he applied for a license, they wouldn't give him one because he was dead, and dead men can't get a license. Isn't government grand?

It seems like everyone who's had extensive dealings with the government or other large, complicated bodies, has their own horror story of mind-crippling bureaucratic asininity. (We should use the word "asininity" more often; it applies to so much!) Here's our own asinine story: Texas had a program through which medically fragile children could get Medicaid even though their families make too much money to get it through normal channels. In order to qualify as a medically fragile child, among a bunch of other requirements, Luke would need to spend thirty days in a nursing home before he could go to our home. (I have no idea why.) The good news was, if we got a doctor's note, we could claim that being in a nursing home would be detrimental to Luke's health, and we could shorten our nursing home stay to one day. Our problem was that in the entire city of Dallas, we couldn't find a nursing home who would take a baby, you know, because THAT'S NOT WHAT NURSING HOMES DO. The closest nursing home we could find that would take him was a facility two hours away in Tyler, TX. Also, this nursing home wasn't equipped to care for babies (go figure), so we would have to bring our own nurse and medical equipment with us since they would be unable to provide us with medical care.

Okay, so the night we took Luke home from the hospital for the first time, we left Dallas around 8:30 at night in a three-vehicle caravan. There was an ambulance in front with Luke, Rachael, and two EMTs, me in our car (packed full of medical equipment) behind them, and our home-health nurse in her own vehicle bringing up the rear. We drove two hours to a nursing home in Tyler where I wrote a check for a couple of hundred dollars for a room that didn't even have a baby bed. We stayed in the nursing home until it was a few minutes past midnight, so we were there for a "day", then we packed up Luke and drove over an hour to our house in Terrell. We spent less than two hours in a nursing home full of old people just to check a box. It was a long night, and it was asinine, but we got our box checked for the government bureaucracy, and we had our Medicaid.

Little Luke's Big Heart

~

One of the most overused tropes in Hollywood is the scene in which one or both parents get overwhelmed by all the stuff that goes with a baby. I watched a scene just the other day in which a mother finally got her mountain of equipment perfectly in place. The punchline came when her friend walked in and pointed out that in getting all the details right, mom forgot her baby. Hilarious right? Maybe you had to be there. Yeah, I have a hard time watching those scenes after our experience. In order for Luke to move anywhere, we needed to pack him into a special stroller that would accommodate all his baggage. This stroller was so specialized we had to receive training on how to work it. I made the mistake of calling it a wheelchair *once*. Rachael did NOT like that at all. He had a special stroller, not a wheelchair (even though it was totally a wheelchair). At this stage, there was no way Rachael or I could transport him solo. We both had to go everywhere, every time. By the way, we also had to have all the normal diapers, toys, wipes, and everything else every other baby has as baggage. All of this was hard. I get tired just thinking about it, and Rachael fooled with it more than I did.

One final point as we're discussing Luke's baggage. Shortly before we left the hospital, they explained to us that part of going home meant we would need to set up around-the-clock home healthcare. In other words, we wouldn't be going home as a lovely family of three, we would be going home as a lovely family of three plus an endless rotation of ladies in scrubs.

This was difficult for many reasons:

There's No Place Like Home

1. You want to feel like home is where you can fully relax. You know how you feel when company is coming over? It's great, it's fun, and it's nice to be the host. And you know that feeling of *finally* closing the door when all those people go home? I love that feeling. Being an introvert by nature, I generally prefer either being alone or being only with my wife. You know what makes that hard? Having a nurse in your house. You know what's really fun? Meeting a nurse for the first time and having her in the room next to you as you're trying to go to sleep, or do the other things married couples do... like, argue. Where did your mind go? No matter how nice she is, she's still a stranger coming into your house.

2. This was more of an issue for Rachael than for me, but having nurses in our house really blurred the lines of who was in charge of Luke. When we're in the hospital, it's clear that the doctors and nurses are in charge. When we go home, Mom and Dad are supposed to be in charge. When there's a nurse at home, it's tough to tell who really gets to decide on how we're going to take care of our kid. This may sound strange, but remember, at the time, Rachael and I were in our mid-twenties and the nurses were mostly our parents' ages. We were still in the process of developing the confidence we would need to stand up to "real" adults. I think an important part of the developmental process for parents is being fully in charge of another person. We didn't get that for a long time.

3. Home-health nurses are a mixed bag. Typically, we ran into two different types of home-health nurses. The first type was in home-health because they were not qualified to work as a hospital nurse where they could make more money. You really don't want a nurse for your kid who would rather be somewhere else. The second type were nurses who had

worked in a hospital before, but when their life circumstances changed, they wanted the slower pace of only having one patient.

The worst of the first kind was a dreadful girl who blew my mind with her incompetence. Not only could she not measure (a kinda important skill when you DRAW UP MEDS FOR KIDS), but she also poured some of Rachael's breast milk down the sink. I know for some of you that doesn't sound like a big deal, but some of you understand that breast milk is liquid gold, and every drop is precious. I escorted that particular nurse out of our home immediately, and we never saw her again. Here's another horror story. One night around 2 AM I heard the front door open. I looked out on the front porch and saw the lady who was supposed to be monitoring my child taking a smoke break instead. I let her back in, but in retrospect, I should have just thrown the deadbolt, pitched her stuff out through the window, and let her explain to the nursing agency why her shift ended early. Okay, just one more horror story. Early one morning Rachael went into Luke's room to check on things, and lying on the floor beside him, on a pallet she had made with cushions from our couch, was his nurse fast asleep. You may not know this (I didn't until we had nurses), but if a nurse falls asleep on her shift, that's far more serious than if I snooze at my desk in my office. When a nurse on shift does it, it's legally child abandonment, and she's supposed to lose her license. Permanently. Not only had this nurse fallen asleep, but she did it intentionally. I caught two other nurses sleeping in the following years, but they were upright in a chair. Totally different.

And yet in spite of the bad experiences, we also had a handful of nurses we loved dearly and were blessed by. They became a valued part of Luke's life. We still keep up with a couple of them to this day. Good home-health nurses are worth far more than the meager salaries they earn. Once we weeded out the sludge and found the gold, they truly made life livable. I resented having them at first, but quickly learned we could not have kept Luke at home without them. Thank you, Lord, for good nurses!

All right, just so this chapter doesn't feel like a "woe is me" chapter, I'm going to end with two positive applications.

In the first place, even when it's hard, your kid is worth fighting for. I learned a lot about having uncomfortable conversations with people in this season of life. While I still avoid conflict like the plague, I learned that when your kid's welfare is on the line, you will do whatever you must to get him taken care of.

In the second place, you're stronger than you think you are. This means you don't know what you can do until you have to. Learning to live with all of Luke's baggage was one of the more difficult things we've done in life, but when we didn't have a choice, we did it. Even though we took a little longer to get there, eventually we settled down into a nice rhythm, and the baggage didn't seem so heavy.

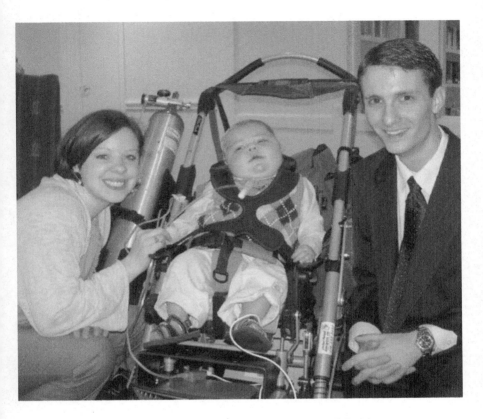

Luke in his "special stroller" (not a wheelchair)

CHAPTER 9

Church People: The Good, the Bad, and the Ugly

Therefore encourage one another and build each other up, just as in fact you are doing.

I Thessalonians 5:11

Don't tell anybody, but my office administrator has a brilliant plan to make a sitcom called *Church Office*. It's basically like *The Office*, but instead of making fun of all the weird people you work with, it makes fun of all the weird people you encounter in church world. And let me tell you, if you're in church world for very long, you will run into a few unique individuals. Once a guy got mad at me because I mentioned in a sermon that I didn't believe in aliens coming to Earth in UFOs. He didn't believe in UFOs either, but he thought I *might* have sounded offensive to his UFO believing father-in-law, a man whom I had never met, seeing as how he didn't go to our church. Another gentleman got into a verbal confrontation with me because he ran the soundboard, and when people would come forward at the end of a service to talk about their struggles, prayer requests, or other personal needs, I wouldn't let him listen in over my lapel microphone (seriously). That was HIS microphone, and I was NOT supposed to hit the off button until after he was finished listening to all my private conversations. I have numerous other stories I could tell you, but for the sake of the weirdos involved in the stories who might read this book, I'll have to keep them on the DL (for now).

Churches tend to attract more than their fair share of odd people[2], but they are also the absolute best place to find an extended family who will love you unconditionally. If you're not part of a loving church family that's living for God and serving its neighbors, you need to join one. Numerous times on our journey with Luke I told people, both in personal conversations and from the pulpit, that I don't know how anybody can go through a serious life-difficulty without a church family at their back. We had a group of Christians who simply because of our common bond in Jesus, loved us and supported us when we desperately needed it. That is the church at its best. In fact, even if you don't believe in Jesus, I would

---

[2] Here's the thing, in every group of five or six church people, one of them is a weirdo. So take a minute and think about the groups you are a part of at church. Got it? If you can't immediately name the weirdo in the group...I might have some bad news for you. The good news is, at church, we love you anyway.

encourage you to get connected to a group of Jesus-people, because at some point on your journey you will need extended family support. A loving church will give it to you with no strings attached. I *love* the church.

Here's an example of Jesus-people love: I can still remember where I was standing in the church parking lot when I told our brand-new youth minister that Rachael and I were heading to the hospital because Luke would be born the next morning. He told me, "Remember that we're with you. You're not going through this alone." (His name was David, and he's from Oklahoma. I'm convinced you can't go wrong hiring a minister from the Sooner State with the name David.) I know it was a Christiany kind of thing for him to say, but it meant a lot to me. I knew I had a bunch of people in my corner.

I remember another occasion months later when things really didn't look good for Luke. The worship leader of our church organized a prayer meeting. Dozens of people showed up on a random night of the week, sat in a circle in the gym, and took turns praying for God's intervention in the life of my son. That particular congregation wasn't big on women praying in public, but when those women started praying from their hearts in the power of the Spirit, there's not a single person on this earth who could have heard those prayers and objected to them. It was awesome, and I don't use that word flippantly. These Jesus-people held our hands, cried with us, and *prayed*.

I don't know when you're reading this, but as I'm writing there is a debate going on across America about whether it's helpful to offer "thoughts and prayers" after a tragedy (in this case it was a school shooting) or not. Those opposed say, "We don't want thoughts and prayers. We want tangible changes so nothing like this ever happens again!" And while I'm all in favor of tangible changes, please don't discount the power of those thoughts and prayers. I can't begin to tell you how meaningful it was to know about the countless people who prayed for my son. As the months moved on, Rachael and I heard from people across the country who knew of Luke and prayed for him. I'm convinced God hears those prayers, and they really do matter.

On another occasion, the church took up a special offering to help with the financial burden that comes from living in the medical world. It was a wonderful gift with many contributing, but the person that day who gave the most in God's eyes was a young boy (Carter!) who brought his piggy bank to church with him because he felt Luke needed the money more than he did. We were at the hospital that Sunday, but we heard there wasn't a dry eye in church as he poured out his nickels and dimes. (No, I'm not crying right now, it's just dusty in here. Seriously.) I can't tell you how many other people on various occasions gave us money, or gift cards, or came and visited, or helped us with things we needed. I can tell you it was a lot, and every card, visit, and donation helped. We had a Jesus-family with us when we needed it.

~

Pardon me for a moment as I move from storyteller to preacher. In most churches, we call our formal, senior leaders either "elders," "pastors," or "shepherds". As you can tell from a couple of those words, the overwhelming leadership model laid out in scripture for leaders is that of a person who herds sheep. The most famous of the Psalms, Psalm 23, describes God as a shepherd. King David, the greatest king of Israel, worked as a shepherd before his coronation, and Jesus describes himself as the "Good Shepherd" who lays down his life for his sheep. God is serious about this shepherding thing as he describes leading. In case you don't know, it's not a flattering metaphor for all of us being led. Sheep are notoriously, well, bless our hearts, to put it delicately, idiots.

On a few occasions, I've spoken to a congregation preparing to select additional leaders. And like a good little preacher, I hammer the shepherding metaphor hard. My first text here is Ezekiel 34. Through Ezekiel, God preaches against the shepherds of Israel for several reasons.

1. The bad shepherds used all the resources for themselves. Good leaders think about how they can serve others, not how they can enrich themselves. If the parents of a family drive nice cars but the kids go to school in rags, then the parents are doing it wrong. Likewise, if the leaders of a church take care of themselves and not others, then they've lost the way of Jesus.

2. The bad shepherds didn't strengthen the weak. The focus of a leader shouldn't be on the strong people who are doing well. It should be on "the least of these" who need help. I've got two kids, one's healthy, and the other has special needs. Guess who gets more help? You know why? Because he needs it.

3. The bad shepherds didn't care about a lost sheep. The job of a leader is to not lose anybody! If you were the adult sponsor on a school trip and lost a kid, there would be a bit of an issue. I don't care how good of a time the kids had, or how good of a job you did staying on budget, it just takes

losing one of the kids to make the trip a failure. I guarantee that if you lose a kid, that's the last trip you get to chaperone. And finally, …

4. The bad shepherds ruled harshly and brutally. This one's pretty self-explanatory. If you want to be like Jesus, words like "harsh" and "brutal" shouldn't come from the lips of your underlings.

Okay, this book isn't on leadership, and there are a lot of other leadership qualities scripture talks about in several other places that didn't make my list. The reason I share this is that I've known some really great shepherds in the church, and I've also known leaders whose negative example could have provided the material for Ezekiel 34. And when you go through a long, traumatic experience, it becomes easy to see who the genuine shepherds are, and who's a wolf in sheep's clothing. [3]

I won't name names, but I'm thinking about one of our shepherds in particular who never came to the hospital, never called us, never prayed with us, and never asked us how he might help. He wasn't interested in that kind of leadership. After all of that, how much trust did I give him to lead me in anything? How much respect did I have for him when he gave me advice or proposed ideas for the church? How likely was I to agree with his point of view in future leadership meetings? Right. Just so you don't think I'm trying to hurt the church he was at, he's not there anymore, and I don't know where he ended up. He didn't last long as a church leader though.

---

[3] In case you didn't know, the metaphor "wolf in sheep's clothing" comes from the teaching of Jesus. He uses the phrase to talk about bad leaders of God's people. See Matthew 7:15–20.

Church People: The Good, the Bad, and the Ugly

On the other hand, I'm thinking about several people who absolutely shepherded us when we needed it. Numerous men and women came and prayed with us, strengthened us, and loved us. Some had official leadership titles, but most didn't. How much respect did I have for those people when they later gave me advice or proposed ideas for the church? How likely was I to see things from their point of view in the future? How much love grew in me for them? Absolutely.

My point is that you don't need a title to be a spiritual leader in God's kingdom. "Shepherd" is not a prestigious appointment. It was actually an occupation held by lower-class people in the ancient world, and I think that's part of why God chose it. In the Kingdom of God, we shouldn't chase titles or positions of power. Personally, as someone who's completed a doctorate, I'll admit it feels good and strokes my ego when someone calls me "Dr. Chisholm," but that's exactly why when people ask me what they should call me (more on that below) I'll usually tell them, "David" or "Dave." If you need a title to boost your ego, you're doing it wrong. "Shepherd" is a title of service and sacrifice so that those who hold it can help us walk in the way of Jesus.

Do you really want to gain influence and take on a leadership position? Figure out who's weak around you that you can love in the name of Jesus and love them. Who's hurting that needs help? Who's struggling? Who needs your love and encouragement today? Are you looking for opportunities to be Jesus to people? If you'll ask those kinds of questions and lead like that, then I guarantee people will follow. You may or may not ever get a title, but through God's power, you can be a shepherd.

Little Luke's Big Heart

~

I have a love/hate relationship with church leadership meetings. (In my particular strand of Christianity, we historically call them "Elders' Meetings.") The reason I don't mind letting you know about the "hate" part is that I'm fairly certain anyone who's been a part of those meetings would support my position. Let's start with the good though. The good part of these leadership meetings, and the reason they exist, is that awesome things can happen at them. We dream about and envision our futures. We pray over our hurting families. We strategize for reaching out to our community and equipping our members for service. We refine our vision and priorities. On many occasions, I've witnessed God move in leadership meetings. At their best, these meetings assist a congregation in moving forward as part of the Kingdom of God. But there is also a bad side to these meetings. They can easily become bogged down by trivialities, or by insanely boring necessary things. (I know what it feels like to be Ferris Bueller sitting in Ben Stein's economics class.) These meetings also tend to be the place where we discuss some more unpleasant aspects of church life. Examples would be hard discussions we need to have with a church member, conflicts we need to work through, or ministries that need retooling. While I'm currently blessed to work with a leadership team that functions with a great deal of maturity, in the past I've witnessed church leaders yell at each other, tear each other down, and even leave in protest. At their worst, these meetings cause active harm to the body of Christ.

Church People: The Good, the Bad, and the Ugly

Likewise, I have a love/hate relationship with social media, and Facebook in particular. And I am including social media in this chapter because it is how we kept so much of our church family informed. Here are my personal rules for what I do NOT post on Facebook (disclaimer—I know there are exceptions to all these rules, but let's be honest, the one you're thinking about posting probably isn't one).

1. Political arguments. Do you really think that if you post that headline with your pithy comment in just the right way you will change anyone's mind? I'm going to go out on a limb and guess you're not a political expert, and all you're doing is reposting stuff you read somewhere else. Facebook is not a good forum for nuanced discourse, and the arguments tend to degenerate into oversimplified talking points. The best you can hope for is that everyone who already agrees with you will cheer, and everyone who favors the other side of the aisle will think less of you. Is that what you're going for?

2. Your dinner. If you're Bobby Flay, Gordon Ramsay, or Rachael Ray, then please post pictures of your food. If you've ever won *Iron Chef*, you can post pictures of your food. If you run a restaurant, you can post pictures of your food. But if you grilled cheese and put a piece of parsley on top of it, you're not a chef, and I don't care to see it. If you ordered something cool at a restaurant, instead of taking pictures for nobody to care about, eat it before it gets cold. I don't care how beautiful the plate looked at Cheesecake Factory—unless *I'm* sitting down in a Cheesecake Factory and the plate in question is sitting in front of *me*. One exception to this rule is if you royally mess up your dinner. If you're posting an expectation vs reality pic, that's Facebook gold.

3. Anything else I find annoying. I know that's rather vague, however, I constantly see a host of Facebook posts that don't fit into the above two categories but force me to rethink (again) deleting the app off my phone. This includes commercial solicitations, scripture verses taken out of context, over-bragging, over-complaining, general whining, and sappy pictures of Jesus asking for a copy/paste. I could include more on this list, but you get the idea.

And yet even though social media has a dark side, it helped us tremendously as we navigated the early years of Luke's life. In the first place, there were so many people who wanted to know the latest on his condition, that there was no physical way we could call and update everyone. It was wonderful to have a forum where we could post an update and know all of Luke's followers would see it. (Shout out to my cousin Clarissa who took most of the Facebook updates and created a blog out of them for us!) Facebook was a vital tool for prayer. Anytime we needed to mobilize Luke's prayer warriors, we could post a request on Facebook and immediately get hundreds of people interceding to God on our behalf. That's powerful. It was also great for posting pictures of Luke. Everyone wanted to see Luke, but when he was in the ICU, we couldn't always have visitors. We were also trying to limit his exposure to all the viruses and germs that well-wishers might bring. Posting pictures on Facebook allowed everyone to see him at an infection-safe distance and allowed us to show off our kid like all new parents want to. Just in case you don't know, NEVER go visit someone in the hospital, especially a little kid, if you are sick AT ALL. Your body can fight off stuff they're not equipped to deal with.

Church People: The Good, the Bad, and the Ugly

One final piece of advice as we close up this part of our discussion: *Don't look it up on the internet.* One day Luke's pulmonologist came into Luke's room and told us about some things going on in Luke's body. He used a lot of medical jargon I didn't understand, so I asked him to repeat several of his words. I asked him how to spell the word on a few terms he used. I'm notoriously bad at spelling, and with medical stuff, just forget it. The doctor spelled it for me, but then he looked me straight in the eye and said, "Don't look it up on the internet. If you have questions, ask us." Before he left, he even repeated it, "I really mean it. Don't look it up on the internet." So, of course, as soon as he left, what did I do? I looked it up on the internet because I had questions.

Now, there are several problems with looking up stuff on the internet. In the first place, most of the good medical articles online are written by and for doctors. Normal people can't understand what we're reading in these articles anyway. On top of that, the parts you can understand don't exactly apply to your kid's situation. Every patient is different, so who knows if what you're reading even matters for your kid? In the second place, much of the stuff online is dated information, and your doctor isn't even thinking in the same world as the article that's based on information from who knows how many years ago. In the third place, and most importantly, much of what you'll find online is worst-case scenario stuff that will not be your reality. All you'll succeed in doing is terrifying yourself. Turns out the lung doctor was right; don't look it up on the internet!

CHAPTER 10

Down, But Not Out

The end of a matter is better than its beginning, and patience is better than pride.

Ecclesiastes 7:8

Whenever you take a breath, whether it's through your nose or mouth, your body does an excellent job of adding heat and moisture to that air so it's exactly the way your lungs like it. However, when a person has a trach, incoming air bypasses the normal route and comes in cold and dry. To help this, they make a little filter that fits over the end of a trach tube called an HME which holds heat and moisture in it to create a more pleasant breathing experience. You can do a Google image search if you want to see the varieties of HMEs available. The ones Luke used were about an inch long and snapped onto the end of his trach like a Lego piece. Luke wore these from the time he was about six months old until he was three and a half. Everybody with me? So far, so good.

Now, for those of you who are parents, have you ever done the thing with your baby where they throw a toy on the floor, you pick it up, and they think, "That's great!" then throw it again? You do that a bunch of times until you finally realize, "Hey, this kid is training me more than I'm training him!" Sooner or later, you get smart, ignore their next missile and settle into a battle of wills? With my second kid ignoring him worked great. He threw a toy down a few times, I quit picking it up, he cried, I smiled, and before long, he learned to quit throwing toys on the floor. I may be a slow learner, but I do get there, eventually.

With Luke, this game was much harder because he quickly learned that if he jerked off his HME and threw it across the house, we would go get it *every time*. After all, the kid needs it to breathe properly, so it's kind of a big deal. Luke trained us from an early age to fetch anytime he needed attention, didn't want to do something, or just felt like watching us run. How do you untrain that?

When he began walking, we did the normal parent thing of baby-proofing the house as much as possible, so we put up a baby gate to keep him out of the kitchen. Luke, however, decided the sound of an HME clinking across the kitchen tile was way cooler than the sound of one hitting the living room carpet. So, with surprising regularity, he would toddle over to the baby gate, pull off the little plastic filter, then grin with delight as his piece of medical equipment flew through the air and headed in for a landing on the hard kitchen floor.

Down, But Not Out

At church, it was even more fun for everyone. While it's annoying to fetch HMEs all over your house, it's even more so to see one sailing through the air mid-prayer or praise song. We always kept a sharp eye on Luke, so most of the time we'd snatch the HME out of his hands before he disrupted worship, but usually about once a service he'd be quick enough to fling it away before we grabbed it. Our regular worship leader got into the habit of just calmly picking an HME up off the floor whenever there was a break in the singing and walking it over to our pew. I'm thankful he was so chill. Luke's best HME throw ever hit the guy praying over the communion one Sunday. I got to wait until the plates passed, then took my personal walk of shame to the middle of the auditorium to complete the game of fetch. The congregation, of course, thought this was hilarious. Rachael and me? Yeah, not so much.

This next part is a little gross, so bear with me. Whenever Luke threw one of those small HMEs and we couldn't find it quickly, we'd simply get out a new one. Then, we'd have to throw away a handful of old HMEs every time we cleaned house. The grossest part was when we packed up to move to Georgia. Every time we moved a dresser, a bed, or another piece of large furniture, we'd find old forgotten HMEs scattered in all the places we couldn't reach. One of the biggest mountains we'd have to climb was the process of getting Luke to breathe without the annoying trach, so we would no longer need to play chase the HME.

Little Luke's Big Heart

~

I'm of the opinion that most books should be short-stories, most short-stories should be articles, and most articles should be tweets. People have an unfortunate tendency to make things longer than they need to be. The old joke is that with some people, if you ask what time it is, they'll tell you how to make a watch. I used to work with a guy who, when asked what time it was, would tell me a LONG story about how he came by his first watch. I worked with another guy who would answer the same question with a condescending mini-lecture about how I should get a watch. I don't want to be those guys. I want to be the guy who will just shoot straight and tell you what time it is.

I write this ironically long intro to say that I don't want to give you a full play-by-play of Luke's hospital journeys for several reasons. It would take way too long, it all starts to sound the same, and with just a few stories, you will get the idea. Overall, Luke had about thirty surgeries, five or six of which I would call major (always a subjective term, because when it's your kid, it always feels major). He had three open-heart surgeries to reroute his blood flow to bypass the right side of his heart. He had more heart caths, scopes, and other procedures than I can count. Luke's laryngotracheal reconstructions, or LTRs for short, are two other surgeries I considered major. We've already talked about his first heart surgery. The only other one I feel the need to discuss in detail is his second LTR.

To explain it simply, before Luke was born, the right side of his heart ballooned to an extraordinary size because a valve didn't form properly. On his earliest x-rays, after he was born, you could see that his heart extended all the way across the top of his chest. Several of his doctors said they'd never seen one that big before. This crushed his airway and caused the cartilage that should hold everything open to not do its job. As long as his trach was in, he could breathe fine, but without it, his airway completely collapsed. To fix this with an LTR, a surgeon takes cartilage from elsewhere in the body (in Luke's case from his ribs) and then uses that to hold open the trachea. Luke's airway was so messed up that they had to do this on two different sections to make it possible for him to breathe with no plastic assistance.

Here's Rachael's Facebook post from August 2012 as we prepared for his second airway reconstruction:

Since we heard Luke would have to undergo another LTR, I've been anxious to get the show on the road, but dreading it at the same time. Dreading it for Luke's sake, but also for my own. This may be selfish, and don't get me wrong, it's excruciating to know your precious child is scared and in pain and there is NOTHING you can do to make it better. I've been very afraid of the personal emotional trauma that is walking down the ICU hallway into my baby's room. The sight of the ointment they put in his eyes after surgery, the cool temperature of his little body, and smells of rubber gloves and anesthesia (yeah, anesthesia has a smell) are very real triggers that make me want to panic and throw myself out the nearest window. I don't though. I take a deep breath and jump in. I talk to Luke, and those words are as much for me as they are for him: "You're so brave. You're so strong. You did great. I'm so proud of you." And in the moment, as proud as I am of his courage and his tenacity, I'm proud of me too. For being here again and not falling apart. For holding it together. For not going crazy.

On the other hand, in a strange way, returning to the CV-ICU has a weird sense of homecoming to it. I'm having to reorient myself to the jargon and the rules. We just got back this afternoon, but I have an unexpected urge to welcome newcomers. My parents-in-law and I met a grandparent couple in the waiting room whose granddaughter was born yesterday. The look in their eyes is so reminiscent of the way I felt when Luke was born: fear mingles with confusion, relief, resentment, bewilderment, and anger. You don't know what's going to happen next, you don't know one end of the hospital from the other, you fret over every beep and alarm, and you stumble blindly over the medical jargon. I want to tell them that it's going to be alright, that they'll get used to the newness and they'll be experts soon enough. But I don't want to sound like a know-it-all, and of course, I don't know that it's going to be alright for them.

The surgery itself was uneventful, and we settled in to wait a few days before his airway healed enough for them to take out his breathing tube. This meant a few days of sedation, after which we would wake him up, take out his breathing tube, and shortly after that, we'd go home with a trach free Luke who could breathe on his own! I can't describe for you how much we were looking forward to throwing away his trachs, suction machine, and all the stuff we had to take with us everywhere we went just to make sure he could breathe. Extubation day was to be a day of celebration.

You'll have to forgive me, but my memories of what happened next, when they took out his tube are not completely clear, and we're still not exactly sure what happened. When they woke Luke up on extubation day and took out his breathing tube, his right lung (the good one) collapsed. When that happened, Luke completely shut down. His left lung has never been awesome since his heart crushed it before he was even born, and it didn't inflate until several days after his birth. What followed was over two chaotic hours of the doctors working on Luke trying to stabilize him. Rachael and I stood in the hallway and watched as the pulse ox numbers on the monitor dipped down into the single digits, his heart struggled to pump, and no matter what they tried, they couldn't get him back. Eventually, they rolled in crash carts and climbed on top of him to do CPR. To this day I can still see the doctor climbing the hospital bed and doing chest compressions on my little three-year-old.

While this was going on, the social worker and the chaplain came and stood on either side of us. They were ready to catch us if/when the doctors decided they could not revive him. They tried to get us to go to the waiting room, but unless they physically moved us, there was no possible way we were leaving. Eventually, my minister friend, Robert, showed up and stood with us too. Finally, two hours later, Luke stabilized.

Two hours is an eternity to try to stabilize a child. After a period of time, I remember feeling the weight of thinking this would be how it ends. After all the struggles, surgeries, therapies, and months in hospital rooms, this would be how Luke's story closed. And then, as it stretched on longer and longer, I worried that even if they were able to get his heart and lungs working again Luke's personality and all the things that made him an awesome kid, would be forever lost. I feared our next conversations with the doctors would be about when it was humane to turn off the machines and let him go. Without reservation, those two hours were the hardest and longest two hours of my life. Just so you don't think I'm overselling this, the head doctor himself later told us that what happened to Luke was as intense as it gets, and that guy's been through it. The only reason Luke didn't die on the table that day is because God intervened. I don't know why God chose to save my son, but I thank him every day that he did.

About a week later they were ready to try extubating him again, and this time everything flowed smoothly. For the first time since he was born, Luke breathed like a champion with no plastic assistance! Luke cried, Rachael and I cried, and I'm pretty sure every doctor, nurse, and therapist on the floor let out a huge sigh of relief. (The crash carts were close, just in case.) It also took a few days to get Luke all the way off his narcotics (sitting with a three-year-old in drug withdrawal is no fun), but once we did, Luke resumed his Luke-ness of joking with doctors and flirting with nurses. (I don't know where he gets *that* from.) Thank you, Lord, we had our little boy back!

~

When *Saving Private Ryan* came out in 1998 I was 15, and a buddy and I decided to go to our local theater to see it. (Don't ask me how I got into a rated R movie at 15; it's not important to the story.) As we're sitting in our seats (pre-stadium seating days) waiting for the previews to start, a group of five or six old men came and sat in the row immediately behind us. Before the movie started, I heard those guys talking to each other about how they remember what it was like WHEN THEY WERE STORMING

Down, But Not Out

THE BEACHES OF NORMANDY. So, check this, I was about to watch the most realistic depiction of D-day ever done on screen, and right behind me was a row full of guys who remembered it personally. For them, it wasn't just a movie, it was a memory. I still have no idea how they sat through it (they're stronger than I am), but when it was over, they got up and left in absolute silence. Ever since that day I've wondered what watching that movie was like for those guys. Also, if you've ever been in the military, thank you for your service.

I'm not a psychologist, nor am I qualified to diagnose anything, but Rachael and I both feel like we had something akin to PTSD after Luke almost died. Out of nowhere, I'd suddenly have the memory pop up of the doctor doing chest compressions. For a long time, my nightmares featured Luke dying in different ways. Now, what many soldiers go through after seeing the horrors of war is on a completely different level than what we experienced, but it's along the same line. You don't watch something like what happened to our son or what happens in war without it leaving a scar.

After that experience, Rachael and I can no longer watch medical dramas. I loved watching *ER* with my mom as a kid, but I can't handle anything close to that today. Once, we were watching an episode of *The Mentalist*, and the main character almost drowned. They have a twenty-second scene of doing CPR to revive him that came out of nowhere. As soon as it flashed on our TV, Rachael broke down. Around the same time, I was sitting in a class in which we watched a movie that climaxed with a woman getting CPR in the hospital. I had to leave and go call Rachael so she could put Luke on the phone and let me hear his voice.

I'll give you two applications from this experience:

Little Luke's Big Heart

1. If you've been through something traumatic, know that it *does* get better with time. The last time I was caught unaware with a dramatic medical scene on TV (in *Stranger Things*) it still hurt, but I was able to move on much more quickly.

2. If you're friends with someone who's seen something that dramatic, know that it doesn't take much to mentally put them back in that life or death moment. Because of what we went through, it took me three days to write out the LTR story. I just couldn't do it in one sitting.

~

A few months ago, we had a garage sale, and while we made almost no money, what we did get was glorious, blessed, empty space! We have closets that look much better, and the most exciting part is that I now actually have room to walk around my car in my garage. Again, I'm not qualified to give psychological advice, but if you feel your life is too chaotic, pick a room or a closet in your house that's full of junk and clean it out. The rest of your life will just plain feel better.

Immediately upon going home from the hospital with a trach free kid, Rachael and I got out a couple of big cardboard boxes, we loaded up all his trach paraphernalia, and I drove forty-five minutes into Dallas to donate it to his pulmonologists' clinic. I wanted it out of my house, and out of my life. I can't describe how euphoric and cathartic Rachael and I felt to get rid of all that crap. We felt a hundred pounds lighter knowing we didn't have to carry around his suction machine, extra trach tubes, and all the other little things that are a part of living with a kid on a trach. We couldn't fully believe it for a while, but eventually, we even decided it was safe to get rid of his suction machine. (You can't donate those.) Throwing that thing out felt so good I even took a picture of it laying in the dumpster.

One more piece of advice I have for those who may be struggling with a medical kid is to celebrate your victories. Every time Luke gets to simplify something about his medical life, we celebrate it. As I write this, we just got back from a cardiology appointment in which the doctor told us we could discontinue one of the meds Luke has been on for his entire life. That means when we made it home from the hospital, we celebrated. Whenever we lose a piece of medical equipment, we celebrate. One thing that sticks out to me as I read the gospels is that Jesus knew how to eat, drink, be merry, and celebrate. If we're followers of Jesus, we don't need much of an excuse to have a party. Have you reached a milestone or had even a minor victory? Celebrate!

I put this picture here because it's cuter than the one of the suction machine in the dumpster.

CHAPTER 11

Adults Say the Dumbest Things

And we know that in all things God works for the good of those who love him, who have been called according to his purpose.

Romans 8:28

I hate Romans 8:28. Okay, I don't *really* hate this divinely inspired verse of scripture. What I actually hate is how all too often, well-meaning Christians poorly attempt to quote this text as a piece of encouragement to someone who's suffering. (Quoting it poorly *is* a piece of something, but encouragement isn't it.) As we were going through our Luke journey, I can't tell you how many people said something as obtuse and meaningless as "You know that in all things God works for the good!" Or equally helpful, "Well, you know, this is all part of God's plan." as a way of trying to make Rachael and me feel better. *Really*? My child struggling to draw breath each moment as he lies in a hospital in pain is part of God's plan? *That's* your theology? *That's* what you want to come in here and tell me? *That's* going to make me somehow feel better? Try again. Do better.[4]

Let me tell you two problems I see with using Romans 8:28 in this way, and then I'll tell you what I believe Paul is really saying in this text. The first problem is that when we misuse Romans 8:28 we unintentionally minimize someone's suffering. Now, it's possible that someone's suffering isn't a big deal (the other day I witnessed my younger son break down because his balloon popped), so if in a particular instance of suffering I'm enduring something that's not a big deal, I need to suck it up, shake it off, rub some dirt on it, and get on with life. If someone says something ugly to me, like calling me a "Longhorn fan" or something equally insulting, then the pain from it might be very real, but it's not a big deal, and I need to get over it.

It's also possible that someone's suffering is part of something better that God has planned. For instance, God used Paul's imprisonment as a good opportunity to write half of the New Testament. So, if in a particular

---

[4] Warning to you the reader: I get pretty snarky and sarcastic in this chapter. My wife told me "Hey, that's pretty snarky and sarcastic. Are you sure you want that in your book?" I promptly ignored her warnings, and then my editor read this and told me "Hey, that's pretty snarky and sarcastic. Are you sure you want that in your book?" I've never been good at throttling back, so I'm leaving the sarcasm as is. Just know that I'm not really angry, and I may be overselling my point just a wee bit. Now that I've completely undercut my own credibility, carry on.

instance of suffering I'm enduring a trial that's part of something better God has planned, I need to view it through a different lens and think about how I can use that experience for God's glory. For example, if I suffer through a struggle with pornography or alcohol or even depression or worry, I can use those experiences to minister to other people who have similar trials, and the kingdom of God, not to mention my own spiritual life, will be better for it.

Sometimes suffering isn't a big deal, other times it's a growing experience or an opportunity for God to do something really cool. But our God doesn't cause evil, nor do I believe he actively causes suffering. I believe we often go through real suffering, and sometimes it's intense. The last thing we need someone else doing is minimizing our pain. If you tell me (especially if you've got healthy kids or no kids) that watching my kid struggle is all just fine because in all things God works for the good, and God will use that struggle for great things in his kingdom, then I'm likely to respond by saying something for which I will later have to repent. Romans 8:28 is not teaching that every tragedy is secretly a good thing in disguise. Don't minimize someone else's suffering.

This leads me directly to problem number two with using Romans 8:28 in this way. It forces us to attempt to find a hidden blessing in each piece of suffering. Don't go up to a Christian in the Middle East who has fled persecution from radical Islamic terrorists, or lost his home, or watched his kids die and his wife get raped and tell him "Don't worry. God works in all things for the good of those who love him! And if you could only see how God is going to use your suffering for his glory, you'd praise Jesus!" Sounds stupid when you ramp it up like that doesn't it? Here's a hint for interpreting scripture: If it doesn't work when you exaggerate it, it probably never works. Now, can God use suffering for good? Yes. Does he regularly get good out of bad? Absolutely. Have we all learned a few lessons from our past sufferings? No doubt. Has God turned a lot of bad things in the world into opportunities for his kingdom to advance? Yep. Does that mean God causes suffering, or that we should rejoice when our child gets sick? No, not even a little bit.

One day I was listening to the local Christian radio station with my kids in the car. Don't judge me, it's the only station I consider safe for them to listen to. When they're older, I'll teach them about real music, or more likely, their mom will. Anyway, they were interviewing a lady whose husband died and left her a single mom with a baby and a toddler. And this woman said that God was faithful in comforting her through her trials. Great. I have no doubt God was faithful and that he comforted her as only he could. Then, bless her heart (BTW "bless her heart" is the southern equivalent of calling her a little slow), she said something that almost made me drive off the road. This sweet lady said, "I wouldn't trade my suffering for anything because God has been faithful through it all." Really? I believe with every fiber in me that God has been faithful, but you're *literally* saying, that given the choice, you wouldn't have your husband beat that disease and have your kids grow up knowing their father? *That's* what you're saying? Given that choice, you would pick dead husband/father because of the lessons you learned through that tragedy? I don't believe it. Not only do I not believe it, but it's not how God works.

I won't take the time to quote it here, but it's worth finding a Bible and reading through Romans chapters 5–8 if you want to understand 8:28 in context. What Paul is basically doing in 8:28–39 is giving a summary of his covenant theology that he's worked out in chapters 5–8. God chose people with Jesus' faith to be his people. He is taking all the Jesus-people to our final destination. We are going to the Promised Land in which he will redeem all of creation, conquer death, and establish his eternal kingdom. Christians, another word for Jesus-people, know where we are going. We get to be on this journey with God because of the death, burial, and resurrection of Jesus. Because the Jesus-people are part of that covenant, there is absolutely nothing that can separate us from God. That's the good news.

Romans 8:28 tells us that no matter where we are in our current journey, we can know God is working on his mega-plan to fix all of creation. We know the mega-plan has a happy ending. Our job, as those who are called to follow Jesus, is to love God and stick with him even though following Jesus is often hard. Paul's next move in the following verses is to say, "Remember, nothing can separate you from God's love." That's the lesson.

So, on the journey of life, you will have highs and lows. You might go through some really intense suffering, and you might go through periods of incredible joy. A lot of life will be quite monotonous. Sometimes you'll be able to see that God is working in your journey. Sometimes you won't. Sometimes it will make sense. Sometimes it won't. But no matter what you face, and no matter what you endure, you can know two things: One, God is in the driver's seat, and two, life is ultimately going to end in glory for the children of God. The ups and downs of life don't ultimately matter, because we know how the story finally ends. That's the good news, and that's totally awesome.

~

Let's imagine you're about to go to the hospital to visit someone whose baby is alive because a whole bank of machines is working hard to keep their little one that way. And you've just read my last section (surely multiple times since it was THAT good) so you know better than to quote Romans 8:28 at them, or, heaven forbid, tell them this is part of God's plan. You're not going to say, "All things work together for good for those that love the Lord" and thereby imply that if only this family loved God more, they could expect a better outcome. You're not going to be that guy or gal who says something thickheaded, meaningless, or incompetent, because you will know better! Now, of course, comes the awkward time when you walk in, give a hug, and then feel an overwhelming urge to say something to kill the silence. So, what do you say?

Before you're ready to graduate to a black belt level chaplain (I did work for a short time as a chaplain, and disappointingly they didn't have different degree belts), I'd like to go over a few more things you shouldn't say when you are in a situation in which you're trying to comfort someone going through a serious, ICU level crisis with their loved one. Ready?

1. "I know how you feel." No, you don't know how they feel. And even if you somehow had a kid with the exact same diagnosis as their kid, their experience is still different from yours. Honestly, right then they probably don't care what you know or don't know. For more minor trials

and sufferings there *might* be a place to say this, but if it's anything major, then saying this simply isn't helpful.

2. "I know you feel alone, but you're never alone because God is with you." Okay, you are *technically* never alone because God is always with you. They know that. But you just invalidated their feelings by telling them they shouldn't feel alone. If they're in the midst of pain, the last thing they need is for you to tell them not to feel what they're feeling.

3. "Let me tell you about a time I was hurting…." Right, because what they want right now is to muster up sympathy for someone else. They do not need their pain intensified by the story you have, and it will not help them feel better. My caveat here is that there *is* a time to share your pain with someone who's hurting. I'm thinking about a guy I know who lost his wife and wanted to talk to someone who had also lost his wife not too many years earlier. *After* the initial pain, it can be helpful to talk to someone who has been through something similar. If this unsolicited "help" comes too soon though, it will only boost the pain they are already in. If the person in crisis wants to talk about your pain, they will be the ones to bring it up.

4. "My friend's sister's boyfriend's cousin had the same thing happen to her, and she died (or, she got better)." If you know someone who died with the same or a similar diagnosis to what their loved one has, then they really don't want to hear it. They've probably already talked to the doctors about survival rates, and your anecdote won't add to their knowledge. Further, if you know someone who lived through something similar, then that's great for that person, but you have no idea if that's going to be the same outcome for their loved one. My favorite examples of this were when

people would tell us things like "Oh, your baby has a heart problem? I knew of a kid with a heart problem, and he's now running marathons." Okay, not all heart problems are equal, not all outcomes are equal, and not all cool stories are equally helpful. Please watch what you say.

5. "Here are some Bible verses you should read." I'm a fan of reading the Bible. I have three degrees all aimed at helping me read the Bible better. What's the problem then? Not only does this advice sound condescending, but it also makes the Bible sound like a magic book. If only they would read the passages you've carefully discerned for them, then their suffering would be over. The Bible is a great source of comfort, and we'll talk more about how Luke's journey impacted my faith, but unless the person brings up the Bible, you most likely shouldn't give them a handful of proof-texts.

6. "God won't give you more than you can handle." Again, this may be kinda-sort-a correct. (1 Corinthians 10:13 is about temptations to sin, not about enduring suffering so you would be misquoting the verse.) Basically, you've just told a person in suffering that they should suck it up and walk it off. That won't be very helpful or encouraging to them.

7. "It could be worse." Yep, or you could not be here at all, and things would be better. (Okay, that was super sarcastic, and I don't really mean it. But it was funny right? No? Moving right along....) Nobody really wants to think about things being even worse. It is just not nice to say this to a hurting person.

8. "I have a friend who drank this special herbal tea and it really helped." I'm a fan of tea, and I like essential oils. I am certainly willing to try alternative treatments. If you have a friend dealing with snoring, skin

rashes, or headaches, then by all means, suggest a natural remedy to them before they try a regular medication or have surgery. If you're talking to someone whose heart is missing a valve, please don't suggest that what your friend picked up off the shelf in the tea store at the mall might be able to do more than what a whole team of medical professionals can do. Your friends will know you're trying to help, but unless you went to medical school, don't try to replace their cardiologist, other doctors, and the professional services they offer.

9. "Let me tell you what my preacher said about suffering...." I'm a fan of preachers (well, some preachers), but if your friend is in the midst of suffering, it's not the time for them to hear a theology lesson even if you did go to seminary.

10. "Everything's going to be alright." Unless God has granted you a prophetic vision of the future, this is just wishful thinking. If you don't know their loved one is going to have a lovely outcome, please don't tell them their loved one is going to be alright. You would feel terrible if everything wasn't alright. Fair?

11. "Dude! Did you catch the game last night?" This one's a little tricky. If you visit your friend in the hospital and they bring up a football game, then they want to talk about something meaningless, and it's cool for you to distract them. But if they're upset about their loved one, and you bring up something meaningless like sports, politics, or the weather, then that sounds like you're not taking their problem seriously enough.

12. "So who's handling X, Y, and Z at work?" This one is the flip side of number 11. If they don't want to talk about something meaningless, then they certainly don't want to talk about meaningful problems that are

now completely outside their control. They don't need anything extra on their "to do" list or anything else to worry about. They might well need to figure out who's handling the meeting on Wednesday, but right now, they're focused on making sure their kid is breathing. If you know there is something they need to do at work, maybe you could help them and take care of it for them instead of worrying them about it.

Massive disclaimer: I'm not a big fan of absolute lists so please take everything in the above list with the appropriate grain of salt. I've read too many articles with titles like "Ten Surefire Ways to Make Your Church Grow!" More important than the actual words you use when visiting someone in distress is the attitude and tone you bring with you. Be empathetic and caring. Your goal shouldn't be to cheer up the ICU room or make everyone feel better. You're not Jesus (shocker), so don't try to be the savior. If someone is worried about their kid's life, then, as odd as it sounds, they don't want you to make them feel better, they just want to know that they're not going through this scary situation alone.

One more thing before I give you my list of stuff you can and probably should say: When you're talking to someone in distress *you don't have any answers*. If someone asks the "why" question (Why is this happening to me/my loved one?), you don't know. Even if you DO know (Well, Cupcake, you smoked three packs a day, so now you have cancer), in their moment of distress, you don't know. Here's the thing, I'm a minister, and I like to think I have some reasonably good, theologically nuanced, biblically informed, helpful answers to suffering and distress in the world. I thoroughly enjoy being the answer guy who shares his profound knowledge with anyone who will listen, or even just nap in my presence, but answering the "why" question is not usually helpful or even very informative. Maybe later, after the initial shock is over, it can be helpful to study a few Bible teachings on suffering and brokenness, but please, please, please, don't give pat Sunday school answers to someone in real suffering. Even if you've got a First Place, Third Grade Division, Bible Bowl trophy from '91 (which I do), and you think you're ready to give deeper and more theologically informed answers, just remember that the person asking the "why" question isn't really asking you for an answer anyway.

Here's the thing, nobody ever came to visit us at the hospital intending to hurt us. People genuinely wanted to help. Even when they said the "wrong" things, we knew their hearts were in the right place, and we didn't get upset or demoralized by it. I wrote this to hopefully help you do a hospital visit where after you leave the husband and wife don't look at each other and say, "Can you believe he/she said...?" You don't want to be that guy. What you can and should say (in my not so humble opinion) is one of the following things:

1. "I'm really sorry."

When you say that, you are communicating that you feel bad that they're in the situation they are experiencing. They don't want, or expect, you to feel the same intensity of emotion over their situation as they do (it's not your kid after all), but it's really nice and bonding when they know you feel something.

2. "Tell me about your loved one."

They're living in a world in which their whole life is centered on the next set of test results, or the doctor coming in for his thirty-second rounds, or watching numbers beep on a screen. They *want* to tell you how their kid is doing, either good or bad, so you can understand where they're all at for today. The absolute best question you can ask is "How's he doing?"

Here's a quick example of how this can go poorly. Several years ago, I went to the hospital to visit the family of a church member who was having spinal surgery. It was a delicate procedure, and the family had already been through a lot of medical stuff leading up to this. They weren't exactly in distress, but it was still an anxious situation. I had the bright idea of taking one of the church shepherds with me. (In all fairness, it's not the *worst* idea I've ever had.) This older gentleman had done lots of hospital visiting before, so it should have been relatively straightforward. When we got to the waiting room and met with the wife and kids, he immediately launched into this long narrative about how once upon a time, he had surgery on his spine. (Remember, I'm a preacher. I'm an expert in extensive pontificating, and this guy put me to shame.) Okay, it was a different situation, and even if it had been the exact same surgery, NOBODY CARES. My favorite part, however, was when the surgeon came in to tell the family how the procedure went, and my elder *told his whole surgery story again to the surgeon*. I seriously contemplated asking if there was an anesthesiologist nearby who would come in and knock one of us, either one would work, out of our misery.

I get it. It's sometimes awkward when you go visit someone because you're not sure what to say, and so you start rambling to ensure that (at least on your watch) no awkward silence will prevail. Just remember two things. Listening is a golden skill, and remarkably few people possess it. The vast majority of us listen to our conversation partner (in any situation, not just in trauma) only enough to formulate our own reply. Most people think so hard about what we are going to say next that we never truly listen. But to be blunt, none of us are as interesting as we think we are. In a tough situation, a hurting person doesn't care about your super cool story right now, and if you would quietly listen, your presence would be much more helpful. Supposedly St. Francis of Assisi said, "Preach the gospel at all times, and when necessary, use words." I'm fairly confident that whenever we go and just listen to suffering people, it's the best sermon we're likely to ever preach.

3. "Is there anything I can do for you?" or even better... "Here's something I am going to do for you."

A lot of people asked us this question when we were in the hospital, and we could usually tell when it was a platitude and when someone actually meant it. One wonderful, godly lady did better than the generic question and told us "I'm going to Pei Wei (side note—if anyone has any connections, please get a Pei Wei to come to Georgia), what do you want for dinner? Also, would you rather me stay and eat with you guys, or just drop it off and leave?" This was nice for a lot of reasons, not only for the awesome food, but sometimes we wanted some conversation, and sometimes we didn't want to have to leave our kid to go see a well-meaning visitor. On that occasion, Rachael and I took turns going to the waiting room and eating with this saint because we wanted company AND we didn't want to leave our kid. That's a win.

I remember one evening coming home from being at the hospital all day, and somebody had mowed my yard. He didn't tell me he was going to do it, and even though I figured out who did it through some Sherlocklevel detective work (okay, I asked his wife), he wanted his good deed to remain anonymous. That's good ministry.

Several people from church brought us meals. One lady brought us a bag full of quarters, so we'd be able to use the vending machines at will, and one church lady did our laundry. I forever after this felt weird about knowing she'd folded my underwear, but hey, we're all family, right? And even if ninety percent of the time a family in distress answers your question with "Oh, we're fine, but thank you," by offering to do something, you're communicating tangible love. The biggest needs a family in the hospital have are taking care of chores, food, and especially...

4. "We're praying for you."

Follow through on this one is key. It's easy to tell someone you're praying for them, but it's a whole different level of ministry to actually do it. Please don't let this be something you say as empty words. Let it be a promise you make that you will call on the God of the universe to intervene in the life of my loved one. I know that Luke is where he is because of prayer, so please take it seriously.

I hope the "What Not to Say" list doesn't put anyone off from going to see someone in the hospital and using the "What to Say" list. You can do this! Just remember to listen, keep the visit about them, and most importantly, pray.

CHAPTER 12

Comparisons Will Kill You

Love is patient, love is kind. It does not envy, it does not boast, it is not proud.

I Corinthians 13:4

From our earliest days of consciousness, all of us learn how to navigate through the social circles of life by comparing ourselves to our contemporaries. Comparison is a natural process of growing up. When I played little league baseball in grade school, I measured myself against my teammates. I knew I was the second slowest kid on the team (thank goodness for that one chubby kid) so after a couple of seasons, I figured out I was never going to live out my dream of playing an infielder for the Atlanta Braves. And these comparisons go far beyond athletic prowess. As I grew older, I began to compare my appearance to others and learned that I'm ridiculously handsome. (It's unfair to the rest of you if I'm being honest.) As kids, we compare everything about ourselves to everyone around us, so we can learn how we measure up. That's just life. Unfortunately, most of us never outgrow the comparison mindset. Adults compare their lives to others all the time, whether it's the kind of car we drive, the size of the house we live in, or the prestige of our job. A long time ago we invited a wealthier couple over to our house for dinner. They looked around and said, "Oh, I love your cute house! It's... cozy." Comparing ourselves to others is just something we do. Unless we are well grounded in our identity as a loved child of God, it's also incredibly dangerous.

I remember calling our health insurance company to get some details straightened out once while I was sitting in Luke's ICU room when he was a little baby. I was fortunate enough to connect with a sweet lady who was extremely sympathetic to our situation. She was doing great, but then she said, "Oh, *I know how you feel.* My baby had pneumonia once, and it was really upsetting to me." And I know she meant well. She was trying to identify with me, which is a good move, but she made a terrible comparison. Was her kid on life-support for months and months? Did the doctors tell her that her kid wasn't likely to make it? No? Then she didn't know how I felt and couldn't even begin to compare her situation to mine. I know pneumonia can be quite serious (Luke had it several times), but typically you treat it, you get better, and you move on like it never happened. Don't compare your kid who got sick one time to someone's medical baby. Even if you can empathize, they are not at all the same.

Comparisons Will Kill You

In most of the sick-kid comparison contests, I will win. My kid was sicker than most other kids. Parents with really sick kids may not have much sympathy for other people's situations because our situations were worse. I'm sorry your precious pumpkin had a hard time because of his food allergy. My kid has no option but to get his nutrition through a tube. I'm sorry your baby cried a lot and kept you up at night. Mine *couldn't* cry out loud because he was unable to move air across his vocal cords. We had to take a nurse with us everywhere we went. I hope you didn't! If you compare your baby-raising experience to mine, mine was much harder practically every time. I desperately wish we had experienced only the normal struggles of parenting. I am, unfortunately, good at winning the who's-had-a-worse-experience comparison game. My kid's had about thirty surgeries. Where are you at? Hopefully nowhere close to there.

Here's the two-fold catch hospital life drilled into me though. One, there is no prize for winning the comparison game. And two, as bad as my kid's situation might be, there's always someone doing worse, aka, I always win the comparison game except for when I don't. Here's the story of how that hit home.

When Luke was just shy of his first birthday, he got really sick and ended up back in the hospital. While we were there, the doctors decided it was time for his second open-heart surgery, but they were anxious about it because they didn't want to operate on him while he was fighting off an infection. So, we got him mostly better, and they performed the surgery without giving us a great deal of notice. We were nervous about it, and I could tell that even Luke's medical team was nervous, but they felt this was likely our best window, so we should take it. As I said earlier, you never get used to sending your kid back to surgery.

The surgery went well, and he spent the first night of his recovery in a room next to another heart baby whose parents were a young couple much like us. Because of the way the rooms angle, I could see the door to the next room, but I couldn't see into the room itself. A few hours after everything had settled down and Luke was doing great, Rachael left to go eat dinner while I stayed with Luke. Not long after Rachael left, I could see the activity level increase in the next room. More doctors and nurses were going in and out. Over the next several minutes I felt the energy level steadily rising. It rose to a frantic peak as staff and equipment rushed in and out. I could feel the intensity. Then, all at once, I literally perceived the energy level shatter. I knew in that exact moment, that this baby, who was just like my baby, had died. I saw nurses crying and doctors walking around with grim faces. Rachael came back into our room at that point, and I left to go find dinner for myself. (I hadn't eaten all day.) When I got to the waiting room, I saw one of the doctors go into a side room with the distraught parents of the neighbor baby and the chaplain. Read this next sentence slowly. *While I celebrated that my baby had done better than expected in his surgery, another couple learned that their baby would never go home.*

So, how's my comparison game working now? Here are the truth and the lesson. There's always someone living a harder story than you are. Our journey with Luke has been incredibly difficult, but at the end of it all, we got to take our baby home.

Comparisons Will Kill You

I don't know what Luke's ceiling is. I know he has some developmental challenges, and in many ways, his brother Sam, who's four years younger than he, passed his older brother by the time he was about four. But I also know that Luke's ahead of some other kids at his school. Chances are that some of you reading this have had either a harder medical struggle or have a loved one who's not doing as well as my child, and you can "win" that comparison game. Just remember, there's no prize for winning it, and everyone's story is different.

So, for a long time I would make the drive from the hospital in the heart of Dallas out to our home outside the city, and I would look at the empty seat behind me and think how wrong it was that instead of my son sitting strapped into his baby carrier, he was connected to a hospital bed far behind me in my rearview mirror. I thought about how unfair it was. Lots of other parents were driving around with their families happily intact. But after that baby died in the room next door, I looked at my empty seat, and I thanked God my kid was alive. Please don't compare your story or your loved one's story to somebody else's. Be thankful for what you have and simply walk the path God has given you with faith.

~

As we continue to think about comparisons, I have to skip a few years ahead and tell a NSFC story (Not Safe for Church). You can totally judge me for this one, but I don't care, it's amazing. Once a year Rachael and I have to go to a meeting at Luke's school to discuss how he's doing and what class he should be in. We basically talk through how formal education should work for him. This is a fairly serious meeting as it involves school officials, his teachers, therapists, and even the school nurse. So, we're in this meeting, and Sam, who's not quite four at the time, is sitting on my lap quietly playing on his tablet. Quite suddenly, he hops down, walks over to where Rachael is sitting and climbs up into her lap. About thirty seconds later, he silently gets down and comes right back over to where he started in my lap. As far as I knew, he was doing what four-year-olds do, which is to move around because they can't make up their minds about where they want to be. Turns out, Rachael had a very different experience of the same story. She saw Sam crawl up in her lap, and then grin at her sweetly. She thought, "Oh, my baby needed a snuggle with his mama!" But then, Sam rips out a fairly sizable toot right on her lap, grins at her again, then without a word, comes back over to sit with me. Okay, let this sink in for a minute. My kid totally, in the middle of a serious meeting, changed locations for the sole purpose of farting on his mom. (I told you it was amazing.) I don't know if I've ever been prouder of my son in my life. Of course, when we got to the car, I heard a number of words about how "Your son is just like YOU!" Fair comparison. That's my boy! He's my mini-me.

It's a long, time-honored tradition that kids inevitably turn into their parents. The older I get, the more I find myself doing and saying things exactly like my dad. I remember that as a kid I always thought it was ridiculous that Dad was the light switch Nazi. Any room in which we left a light on resulted in a light switch lesson. He literally would gather my sisters and me into a room, point at the switch and ask, "Does anybody know what this little thing does? Anybody?" But now that I pay my own electric bills, I've suddenly found myself barking out, "These lights cost money! How hard is it to flip a switch on your way out of a room?" My "Oh-no-I'm-my-father" moment really hit me one day as I gathered my two sons into a room and found myself pointing at a light switch. While that's a fairly mild example, I know that for good and for ill, most of us default as adults to whatever example mom and dad set before us. Our marriages tend to look like our parents'. If they yelled, we yell. If they suppressed everything, we probably will too. Our spending habits, work ethics, moral values, political affiliations and mannerisms all tend to look a lot like mom and dad. Unless we intentionally choose to change something, and invest the resources to change it, we naturally turn into our parents.

The flip side of this is that as a parent there are certain things I want my kids to get from me. I want to teach my sons who to root for in college football (Boomer Sooner), how to make a strong opening in a game of chess, how to appreciate fine science fiction, why the best coffee is black coffee, and what the best golf grip is to cure your slice. As a parent, I take a certain amount of pride in my sons acting like me (toots and all). Parents have a God-given inclination to want their children to be like them. In fact, throughout scripture, God uses the metaphor of parent/child and insists that the goal of our life is to become more like our parent, God. The very first story in scripture culminates in how God created humanity. Unlike everything else in creation, God did this by creating humanity in his own image (Genesis 1:27).

How this all bears on the present story is that I don't know to what extent Luke will ever compare to me. I don't know if he will be able to graduate from high school. I don't know if he'll ever have the mental capacity to learn how to play chess and appreciate science fiction, or if he'll have the physical attributes necessary to play golf. He already knows how to yell at the screen during a college football game, but he's simply cheering for the red team. He's continually growing and maturing, but I don't know what his ceiling is.

I consider the grieving process that happens to families of special needs children somewhat unique. In other aspects of life, something bad happens, you grieve over it, and it becomes a part of your history. You might occasionally remember and re-grieve, but that intense moment of pain stays in the past. With a special needs child, the grieving process is a little different because every time you see other kids doing something "normal" it grieves you that your kid is missing out. New "losses" hit the special needs family with great regularity. One day we went to the park and Luke really wanted to play baseball with a group of boys, but he just physically and mentally couldn't do it. He tries to run with his brother Sam who's four years his junior, but he just can't keep up. Sam gets invited to spend the day at a friend's house, but Luke doesn't get those invitations.

As they grow older, I don't know if Luke will drive a car, bring a girl home, or get a job. As his father, I will grieve each of those missed milestones both for his sake, and selfishly, for my own. In so many ways Luke will not be able to be like me.

But as I reflect on how I became so much like my own father, I remember that I followed in his footsteps in more than just light switch lessons. It was from both of my parents that I inherited a strong love for both Jesus and his bride, the Church. A couple of my earliest memories are of Mom and Dad reading me Bible stories and spending time at church as the first ones there and the last to leave. Heck, I even followed my dad into a pulpit. (Can you say "heck" when talking about preaching? That doesn't seem right. Maybe I'll edit that part out before we go to print.) So even though it doesn't take away my grief, I find peace in knowing that whether or not Luke ever learns to swing a golf club or give someone a light switch lesson, if I can teach him to follow me in loving Jesus, then as a father, I've succeeded in the only part that really matters.

~

One final piece I want to get onto the table as we think about comparisons is summed up in the maxim we all know and love to tell our kids—life is not fair. If you know anything about the Myers Briggs personality profile, you know there are people wired with a strong bent towards justice. I'm an ISTJ, and that "J" means that I have a high sense of justice. What's right is right, and what's wrong is wrong. I'm the kind of guy who won't take sixteen items through the fifteen item express lane at the grocery store. I will passive-aggressively glare at those of you who do while I secretly wish the grocery police would send you to the rack for your inability to count too. I really want life to be fair (also, we should have grocery police).

When I was a kid dealing with two sisters, I regularly vocalized all of life's perceived injustices to my parents. "She got a bigger piece than me!" "She didn't brush her teeth like you told her to!" "She touched me!" I was a *fun* kid. Some of you might erroneously think I was a tattletale, but I like to think I was a beacon of justice in a world ruled by anarchy and chaos (you know, like Superman). Life should be fair, and when it's not, I want to do what I can to correct the injustice.

As far as it goes, a desire for fairness is not a bad thing. As a follower of Jesus, I believe justice is an important virtue, and I should care deeply about the poor, the marginalized, and the oppressed like Jesus did. But as an adult, I also know that no matter how much we'd like for it to be different, life is not fair.

As a preacher, I've felt this keenly. Here's my confession—please don't judge me. There have been a few occasions in which I've looked at preachers of churches bigger than mine, and I've thought, "They don't preach as well as I do. That's not fair that they have a bigger church." On the other hand, I've heard some preachers at churches smaller than mine and thought, "Wow. He/she can really deliver it. It's not fair that I'm at a bigger church than they are." Guess what? Life isn't fair. (Not to mention that church size isn't the be-all-end-all of ministry success.) I know that, but I still want it to be fairer than it is.

So, the injustice I now see happening in my life is that I have two sons, and I treat them very differently. I know that anyone with multiple children knows they have different needs, respond to different disciplines, and express themselves differently. You can't help but treat your kids differently. With a special needs child, the differences are much more exaggerated. When Sam has homework, I just tell him to do it. When Luke has homework, I stay with him helping him every step of the way. When Sam doesn't like the food in front of him, I tell him that he can eat his dinner or starve. (He always eats it eventually.) When Luke doesn't like his food, I'll do everything in my power to find something, anything, that he'll eat. When Sam falls and scrapes his knee, I tell him to walk it off and get over it. When Luke takes a fall, I check to make sure everything is okay. My boys are still small as I write this, but I'm keenly aware that the way I'm raising them is not fair, and I can't fix it.

The other day I took the boys to the park. (BTW, when a preacher says "the other day" the story may be anywhere from yesterday to thirty years ago.) I made a big deal out of taking them to the park because Mom needed to work, and we were close to their most favorite park in all of Georgia, which is a park a considerable distance from our house. We don't go to this park often, so the whole way there I talked it up. "We're going to the park that looks like a castle. You guys remember when we had your birthdays there?" They were super excited, and when we arrived, they bolted out of the car to begin their adventure. No more than five minutes later I knew there was a problem with Luke. He'd messed up his pants, and because of an accident he had earlier in the day, I didn't have a spare pair. With great weeping and gnashing of teeth, I took the kids back to the car for the ride home. Sam howled, "I didn't do anything wrong! Can I stay here and just Luke go home?" They both cried the whole way home. And Sam was right. He hadn't done anything wrong. It wasn't fair that because of his brother's actions he would be punished with only a five-minute trip to the park. It's not fair, but it's our life.

In 2017, Owen Wilson and Julia Roberts starred as parents in the movie *Wonder,* which was about a special needs child, Auggie (played by Jacob Tremblay), who goes to middle school and adjusts to life as a "different" kid who tries to fit into normal life. It was a good, heartfelt movie. Rachael and I repeatedly identified with the Owen Wilson and Julia Roberts characters. I'm the cool and funny dad, and Rachael is the all-giving, good-looking mom, in case you didn't pick that up. But the character I appreciated most in the entire movie was the sister, Via (played by Izabela Vidovic). The movie did an excellent job of showing how Via was a normal girl whose entire life became overshadowed by the overwhelming needs of her little brother. Everyone assumed she was okay even though she didn't get the attention she deserved because her little brother took up all the oxygen in any room. It wasn't fair. Spoiler alert, in the movie they all end up as one big happy family. As I look at my own neurotypical kid (I didn't even know they had a name for non-special needs kids until recently), I pray that he somehow understands the attention we give to his older brother. The Chisholm family revolves around Luke, but I pray that Sam will find his own special place in the world. Life's not fair, but we keep trying to make the best of it.

Thanksgiving 2011

CHAPTER 13

Normal Life Is Hard

Therefore do not worry about tomorrow, for tomorrow will worry about itself. Each day has enough trouble of its own.

Matthew 6:34

Where we live, the process for picking up your child from school is rather elaborate. You have to have a number hanging from your rearview mirror that corresponds to your child. That way, after your car snakes through the Disneyland-like line behind the school, they can have your kid waiting at the appropriate spot. Here, they load ten kids at a time into ten cars, so the line keeps moving quickly and all have a wonderful day. It's a great plan. It's a simple plan. But one day, instead of Rachael picking up Luke, I went to get him. When I got through the line, and my car was one of the ten ready to pick up a kid, my child was slowly ambling down the sidewalk, taking in the scenery, with zero concern that the whole school was waiting on him to get to his vehicle. So, in the interest of speeding things up, I jumped out of my car, sprinted down the sidewalk, threw my son under my arm, and bolted back toward my vehicle. As I was running with a kid firmly in my grasp, I made eye-contact with one of the teachers whose job it was to make sure all the children got through the pickup process safely. At that moment, I saw the flaw in my plan. I'd just pulled up to an elementary school, hauled tail up to the closest kid, snatched him off the sidewalk, and was now forcing him back to my car. The look in her eye was that of a mama bear ready to flying tackle me to the ground as she was sizing me up to see how much of a fight I would give her. That's a good teacher. I had to slow down and show her I really was Dad. Fortunately, I didn't have to go home and tell Rachael how I got my butt kicked by the car-line lady. With Luke, even "normal" experiences are anything but.

In our journey with Luke, it's easy to remember all the big mountains we had to climb, such as getting through his heart surgeries or getting his trach out. More common, however, are the new hills we tread daily since every day is a new day in a special needs family. Simple tasks like running to the grocery store or sitting through a church service take on an extra level of complication because Luke just doesn't do anything normally.

When we first moved to Georgia, Luke was four, and Sam was a newborn. Rachael turned her attention towards Sam for just a minute, but that's all it took for Luke to unlock the front door of our apartment and decide he needed to go somewhere. I got a frantic call at my office a few minutes later. Rachael had already screamed her head off for Luke, but he was just gone. By the time I raced home, Rachael had found him wandering around the parking lot, but I had already called the police. Now I had to explain to a very nice officer why he was at our apartment complex looking for a kid that wasn't even lost. The very next thing I did was to install a new lock at the top of the door, safely out of a four-year-old's reach. (The apartment complex never said anything about it either!)

One more story (because it's too good not to share). Once when Luke was eight and Sam was four, we flew back to Atlanta after a trip to visit family. We ended up getting back to the airport well after midnight, and quite understandably, the kids were both tired. Our first stop is *always* the bathroom, so as soon as we got off the plane, I threw Luke onto my back, let Rachael carry Sam, and we bee lined it for the first restroom. Before I got there, however, I felt a nice warm sensation that started about the middle of my back. Yep, at less than a hundred feet from the bathroom, Luke peed all over me. Well, there's nothing for it. I had to carry my son through the entire Atlanta airport (busiest in the world), and then drive an hour back to our house, all covered in urine because my kid still struggles with bladder control.

I'm not complaining, but I could easily tell you a dozen more stories about how normal, everyday things are just harder for us. While things are slowly getting easier, daily life with a special needs child is a different kind of way to live. We've been blessed to have a great deal of support, but I know that not every special family has the same resources we do. If you know a special needs family, don't be afraid to ask what you can do to help. You could be the exact blessing they need at that moment.

Little Luke's Big Heart

~

As a preacher, I regularly run into situations where people don't know what to call me. Once upon a time, I preached a wedding where it was a friend of a friend kind of thing, so I knew hardly anybody there. Over the course of the evening I got called "Pastor," "Reverend," "Preacher," and one guy who bumped into me muttered, "Excuse me, Father." And as it may well be that the closest some people have been to a church service is whatever they've seen on TV, I don't usually correct anybody's title for me. The last thing I want to do is make someone feel like they said it wrong. (I have yet to receive a "Your Eminence," but that would be cool.) For the record, in my tribe, we typically refer to our preachers by a name instead of by a title. One day at the church where I preach, we hosted a Cub Scout troop. One of the moms asked someone what to call me, and the guy said, "Oh him? We just call him David. And that's if we're being nice!"

I tell you that story to ask, have you ever been in a situation in which you didn't know what you should say or do, and so you ended up saying or doing something rather stupid? Once I introduced Rachael as my "first wife" in front of my in-laws. I thought it was funny. They didn't. Or how about an even better story? Once, when Luke was about six months old, we took him to the cardiologist for a checkup. They did the normal thing of weighing him to see if he was progressing properly on the growth chart. For this story to make sense, you have to understand that I have a very slender build. The doctor looked at the numbers and excitedly proclaimed, "Wow, he's really put on a lot of weight quickly!" In a moment of sheer stupidity, I said, "Cool! He sure doesn't get that from his father!" All I meant was that I am skinny, and my kid was getting fat. I didn't think about how my statement implied that Luke received his pound-packing genes from his mother. As the female doctor, the female nurse, and the female I married all turned their vitriolic eyes on me, what I had just said clicked. Yep.

For many people, when they first met Luke, they had that same experience of speaking without thinking. I've already written an entire chapter on what to say and what not to say, so I won't rehash that here, but I will share with you a couple of instances of what happened when people met Luke for the first time.

One of my favorite meetings happened one day when we were transporting Luke from one hospital facility to another to run more tests. I don't remember the reason why, but Rachael couldn't go that day, so one of the nurses, Luke, and I got to take an ambulance ride across Dallas to go to this other hospital. When we got there, the two EMTs wheeled Luke, plus all his equipment, out of the ambulance and through the hospital on a gurney while the nurse and I followed. Now, if you don't know anything about medical equipment, it looks pretty bad. Luke had a tube coming out of his throat and going to a machine that breathed for him. He also had a feeding tube and monitor lines, and so even if you have a little medical knowledge, you can tell Luke is a complicated kid. So, the Luke entourage got on an elevator and shared part of our ride with a dude who looked like he would be right at home on *Duck Dynasty*. He was wearing dirty overalls and had the long, scraggly beard. I could immediately see from his posture that this guy was going to say something. He couldn't help himself. He had a genuine sympathy in his eyes as he looked at Luke, and then me. Then, bless his heart, this old man, in the thickest country accent you can imagine said, "Poor little critter!" Did he just call my baby a critter? As soon as the elevator doors closed, and we left the redneck behind, the EMTs looked at me to see if I was offended. I burst out laughing, they joined me, and we continued on our way.

Another time, when Luke was a little older (four-ish) I took him to a Chick-Fil-A to play on their play place. Chick-Fil-A play-places are nice because, unlike the other fast food play-places, you can take your kid to Chick-Fil-A and they don't feel sticky at the end of their play time. Luke was climbing around, sliding, and generally having a good time when some other boys about his age joined him. They could quickly tell that Luke was different. One boy said to the other, "He's a monster! Run away!" For the next twenty minutes or so, Luke desperately wanted to run and play with his peers, but every time he got close to them, they ran away. Luke wasn't too upset about it, but I had to remind myself that I would get in serious trouble if I punched two little kids. (I was pretty sure I could take them, but I didn't know if I could take their moms.) Part of the reason it broke my heart was that I knew this wouldn't be the last time Luke was on the receiving end of rejection. Kids, and some adults, can be cruel.

Several times when strangers met Luke, particularly after we got out of the hospital and out into the real world, they reacted with a mixture of fear and just plain awkwardness. People didn't know what to do. And I'm certainly sympathetic because, without my experience, I wouldn't know what to think or do either. Aside from the little twerps at Chick-Fil-A, kids were usually the best at meeting Luke. Kids don't know enough to worry about offending you, so they just ask questions. I love it. I don't ever mind answering honest questions from anybody. I know there's something wrong with my kid. I know you're curious. A smile and a question are always okay.

~

When I first started preaching full time in my mid-20s, there was an older man who had never been a preacher who would regularly come by my office, sit on my couch, and give me advice about preaching. Now, I'll be the first to admit that I don't know (and never will know) everything I want to know about the craft of sermon delivery, so I regularly read books and articles, listen to podcasts, and study speeches, all in an attempt to learn more[5]. I am fully in favor of receiving advice and opinions on preaching. I even solicit feedback from members of my congregation. I like to ask questions like "What didn't make sense about that?" and "Did this particular point connect?" etc. My problem with the old man on my couch was not that I was prideful and above hearing advice; my problem was that I had heard him do some limited teaching before, and he was *terrible* at it. I don't just mean he had a bad stage presence (although he did). I mean that he wasn't good at theology, didn't organize his thoughts

---

[5] Some of my favorite 'studies' are good standup comedians. They know how to tell stories and hold attention better than anyone. Jim Gaffigan and Jeff Dunham are two of my favorites. Don't be afraid to learn from someone without theological training. My unsolicited advice to young preachers is to observe how an enrapturing storyteller works a crowd. Also, that way when your wife asks you why you're stuck to the couch watching a Netflix special, you can tell her that you're working.

well, and didn't know how to make illustrations. The guy who wanted to mentor me into better preaching and teaching didn't know much of anything about preaching and teaching. While I appreciated his desire to help me out, I consistently struggled to feign interest as he advised *at* me from across my office.

My point with this story is that with advice, it usually seems that those least qualified to give it are the quickest people to offer it unsolicited. It's the parents whose kids are swimming in the fountain at the mall who want to tell you how to discipline your kids, or the couple who has one kid in jail, another failing out of college, and a third who never keeps a job for more than three weeks; they are the ones who want to tell you how to prepare for the teenage years. It's the guy on his way to pay the pawn shop who gives you financial advice. It's my buddy on the golf course who can't break one hundred telling me my grip is wrong. My grip *is* wrong, but that's not the point. If you haven't had at least a little success in a particular field, then you probably shouldn't be giving advice in that field. The exception to my giving advice rule is politics. All of us with zero experience can all tell those guys how to do their jobs better, right?

Now, if you have a special needs kid, you will receive *boatloads* of advice about how to raise your child; I know Rachael and I did. So, in the spirit of giving unsolicited advice of my own (it is my book after all), I'd like to advise you regarding some issues associated with giving advice to special needs parents.

1. Unless you have a special needs child of your own, you shouldn't give advice to the parents of a special needs kid unless they ask for it.

"The best way to put Luke to sleep at night is…"

"Let me stop you right there. Was your kid hooked up to multiple pieces of medical equipment in his crib? Was your kid lulled to sleep by the sound of beeping machines? Did you wake up your kid for breathing treatments in the middle of the night? Has your kid ever gone into withdrawal from post-surgery narcotics? Ever been on steroids? Ever had a nurse check his vitals every hour for her chart? No? None of those things? Okay, please proceed to tell me how to put him in bed."

Okay, I never had the above conversation, and I never stopped anyone mid-sentence like that, but it's not for a lack of wanting to. I am Dad to both a special needs child and a neurotypical child, and the two experiences could not be more different. Much of the stuff that works wonderfully with your average kid just isn't going to work with a special needs kid. This means that just because you have parenting experience with a normal child, you may not have the history necessary to speak advice into my world. Even if you've successfully raised wonderful, smart, well-behaved, well-adjusted children of your own, your story is so different from the story of medical kids, that whatever comparison you want to make likely doesn't apply. It's like me saying that since I'm a preacher, I can tell someone who's a lawyer how to do their work. Just because we both work with words and people doesn't mean we have the same job.

My caveat here is if you are giving advice as a person of expertise. Luke has had a slew of therapists and psychologists who have worked with him over the years, and they always had great advice to offer us based on their research, training, and experiences working with special needs kids. One of Luke's favorite therapists of all time was a girl named Cherish who was instrumental in not only teaching Luke how to eat but also in helping us learn how to feed him. When she gave us advice on what to do to get him to eat more by mouth, we listened attentively even though she had no kids of her own. Now, expertise comes from years of study (and usually a degree or two). Don't try to say your advice falls into this exception clause because you read an article one time, or saw a great documentary, or had a friend once who had a special needs kid. Watching *Rain Man* qualifies you to give advice on autism about as much as watching *The Mighty Ducks* qualifies me to coach hockey.

2. Please don't give simple solutions to complex problems.

One of our big struggles with Luke has been potty training. We've gotten every piece of advice on that topic you would ever want. One well-intentioned lady told us, "Oh, all you have to do is put cheerios in the potty, and once he sees how fun it is to shoot at them, then he'll want to go." Another told us, "It's all about the sticker chart. Put a chart up in the bathroom, and whenever he has success, he gets to put a sticker on the chart. He'll love it!" My favorite was the recommendation to give Luke M&M's every time he successfully goes (never mind the fact that Luke can't eat solids).

Potty training for Luke was complicated. He had significant issues with muscle tone in his core which made control difficult; we didn't know if his accidents were even possible for him to control. Also, because of his heart issues, he got a lot of fluid regularly and then diuretics to keep everything in balance. We knew potty training would be difficult for him, so we got professional advice from doctors, and therapists, and even read books specifically designed to help parents potty train kids with sensory issues. Potty training was a big problem for us, so we had to throw a lot of resources at it, but then we had to turn around and hear simplistic solutions offered by well-intentioned people who had no idea how complicated this problem truly was. What I wanted to say, but didn't, was "Okay, we've read books, talked to experts, and worked on this for years, but sure, you go ahead and give us your simple life-hack. I'm confident that'll solve it." I'm beginning to accept the fact that I'm something of a jerk.

If you came across a guy on the highway who's pulled over with his hazard lights on and smoke pouring out from under his hood, you wouldn't tell him "Oh, one time my car wouldn't start, and I just needed to put gas in it." Obviously, this motorist has a more complicated problem, and all your "solution" will do is make you look foolish. Your statement might be true, and your intentions pure, but please, don't be that guy.

3. If you're condescending towards me, I'm done.

Nobody likes to be on the receiving end of condescension. An older minister once told me that in preaching, it's important to preach "we" instead of "you". For example, if you want to make a point in a sermon entitled "don't gossip," instead of saying "*you* will face great temptation to gossip, but *you* shouldn't do it," change that to "*we* will face great temptation to gossip, but *we* shouldn't do it." The first way sounds condescending and implies that the preacher is above gossip. The second way makes it sound like we're all on the same level here, and that both the preacher and the congregation should watch out for this particular sin. Guess which way people are more likely to actually hear? (Not that I would *ever* gossip, but you get my point.) My stance as a preacher should not be that of a spiritual expert who's sharing all my profound wisdom with those beneath me; it should be that of a follower of Jesus who's inviting my brothers and sisters to study some spiritual topic or piece of God's word alongside me. This principle applies to more or less everything.

If you're going to give advice to a parent of a special kid, make sure you acknowledge that you don't know or understand, and are simply throwing something out as a fellow traveler. I had a friend once say about potty training, "I know you guys have tried everything, and I know Luke is a special case, so stop me if you've heard this, but something that helped us in our potty-training struggle was using cold water to wash off accidents." Think about how different that sounds from "Oh, you're having trouble potty training? What you need to do is use cold water." The first way comes across with humility and understanding; the second is condescending. Please don't condescend to special needs parents under the guise of helping.

4. Every kid is different.

When Luke first started going to public school he quickly became friends with another special needs boy in his class who had similar surgical history and developmental struggles. Not long after they became friends, we connected with his parents and formed a friendship that's lasted ever since. (By the way, the cutest thing you'll ever see in your life is two five-year-old special needs kids running to hug each other. If that doesn't make you smile, you're dead inside.) Quite naturally, Rachael and I have swapped stories with these other parents, but we pretty much never gave advice to each other. You know why? Because even though this other family had a remarkably similar story to our own, their child was incredibly different. Some things that worked for us didn't work for them and vice versa.

Even if you have a special needs child, I'm probably not going to give you much advice on raising him or her unless you ask for it because your kid is unique. Now, I understand that there are exceptions to this (and everything else in this list), but please, have the humility to think about how you come across to the other person before you start offering advice. Thanks!

~

A couple of years ago Rachael and I, through a mutual friend, became acquainted with a young couple that had just heard the awful words "There's something wrong with your baby." Like Luke, their baby had a heart defect, might not make it to birth, and even if she was born alive would face a series of surgeries. Rachael and I never asked for this to become part of our ministry. If I could have picked from all the possible experiences out of which to do ministry, this wouldn't be it. But this ministry is now part of our experience, so we jumped at the opportunity to sit down with this couple, tell them about Luke, and more importantly, listen to their trauma. This wasn't the first time we met with such a couple, and it wouldn't be the last.

The little girl was born, and everything was going great for her. Then, on the same day she should have gone home from the hospital, she crashed and died quite suddenly. The couple was obviously devastated. On top of that, they didn't have a church family at their back for support. We were the only church people they knew, so they asked me to do the funeral service.

Now I had done many funerals before, and while they are always somewhat difficult, usually the service is for someone who's lived a long life. When they were Christians we also have a sense in which we are celebrating the person's going home to glory. I don't get nervous about funerals, and I can distance myself enough emotionally in those moments to stay professional. But with the service for that little baby girl, it all hit way too close to home. During the slideshow, I recognized every piece of medical equipment and knew how easily this little girl could have been Luke. The parents were military, and I'll never forget what it's like to see a room full of marines in their full-dress blues crying. At the end of the service when they opened the casket, I had to divorce my mind from the moment and go somewhere else. I still came within a hair's breadth of losing it. I don't care how many more funerals I preach as part of my ministry career, that one will be the hardest.

I am telling you this story because I firmly believe God will use whatever struggle you have as an opportunity to minister to others. The best person to run a ministry on pornography is a guy like Craig Gross who launched multiple ministries after his own battle with online addiction. The best person to run a financial ministry is a guy like Dave Ramsey who went bankrupt then learned how to use money and build a business the right way. I don't know what your struggle is, but I know that if you're open to it, God will use you to minister to others.

By the way, knowing that God will use your struggles for greater impact with others doesn't make everything okay, nor does it explain "why" it happened to your kid. This in no way makes it all better. I do firmly believe that God regularly takes even the worst of situations and redeems them for his glory though. While I never would have chosen this particular road to be a part of our ministry, I'm thankful God was able to use us in the lives of a family who lost their little girl.

Epilogue

I fear that in the above chapters I've focused so much on the hard stuff and the stuff that doesn't fit into normal family life, that I've left a skewed impression of Luke. Luke is so much more than a diagnosis. Even with all his (and our) struggles, Luke's life is still mostly consumed with normal, being a kid kind of things. So, in the spirit of giving you a more balanced picture, I want to tell you a couple of stories that highlight this amazing kid's personality.

When Luke was about two years old, I decided to take my wife to Chili's because I know how to show a girl a good time. Okay, the real reason I like going to Chili's with my family is that I don't believe in taking small children anywhere nicer than a place like Chili's. I will judge you if you go somewhere fancy and take your baby or toddler. The possibility always exists that a kid will pitch a fit then need to be taken out. You don't want to interrupt someone's fancy dinner. Not cool. Nobody in Chili's is going to feel slighted if a kid makes a little noise. Also, I'm a big believer in handing my kid a tablet to play with at a place like Chili's in order to keep him entertained while the adults eat and enjoy a bit of real conversation. I once asked my mom how they did restaurants when my sisters and I were little in the pre-tablet era, and she said, "If it didn't have a play place, we didn't go." Fair enough. So, Rachael, Luke, and I went to our favorite casual dining restaurant. Upon entering the establishment, the perky hostess, who might have been eighteen (maybe), grabbed two menus, smiled, and said, "Right this way!" As she turned to show us to our table, Rachael was directly behind me, and Luke was right in front of me, so I could guide him to where we were going. (The order is important—just wait for it.) The hostess turned to show us to our table and Luke reached up and gave her a friendly little pinch right on the butt. Luke then promptly turned his attention back to his tablet in the same instant that the hostess turned around. So, when she turned, she didn't look down at Luke (he's just some kid playing his tablet), she glared at me, and in her expression I could see that she was not only highly offended but was wondering what kind of creep pinches a girl's rump at a Chili's with his wife and kid in tow. I was so surprised I didn't say a word. It was a *long* time before I was willing to go back to that particular Chili's.

Story number two: One of the unfortunate realities for Luke as a medical kid is that he regularly has to get his blood tested. This means he has to go to a clinic, have a tech stick a needle in his arm, and then sit relatively still until he has shed enough blood for that particular sacrifice. I tend to handle blood draws better than Rachael, so I'm usually the one who goes in and helps hold him for this particular procedure. One day, when Luke was eight, and it was a few days before Christmas, I took him into the lab. As soon as we walked in, he knew what was coming (this wasn't his first rodeo) and proceeded to scream his head off until it was his turn. I finally got him on my lap in the chair and, with the help of a lab tech, held him down while the second lab tech did the blood draw. As soon as the draw was complete, he wiped the tears from his eyes, hugged both lab techs, and then without waiting for me headed out the door saying, "Thank you, and have a merry Christmas." Like. A. Boss.

I'm super excited to be this cool kid's dad. Before he could talk, he could read hundreds of words and used sign language to communicate. When he first started talking, we had a lot of trouble understanding him, which frustrated him. Once when we were shopping at Walmart, he was trying to tell me something, but I couldn't make it out. Finally, he looked at me and spelled out B-A-L-L. The kid wanted a ball! He has always loved letters and numbers. We even made him a letter pit in his playroom out of a swimming pool.

I love that Luke loves people. I love that he can light up a room. He also loves long baths, and many mornings he just wants to soak for a while to wake up. Luke loves going to the park. He loves reading books about planets and states and currently sleeps every night on a United States pillowcase. His favorite thing in the world is to FaceTime with his grandparents. He tells jokes, and if one gets a laugh, he'll immediately tell the same joke again. He loves swimming. He's not a big fan of going to school, but he loves his friends (and music class) there. He's a cool kid, and I'm excited to watch him growing up.

Little Luke's Big Heart

~

Most television shows follow a similar pattern in that they open with a problem. The problem ramps up as the characters try to solve it, and then in the penultimate scene there is resolution This leads to a few minutes of closing, and finally, the credits roll. Pop on an episode of *Law and Order*, and you're likely to see a dead body (problem) followed by detectives scrambling to find the murderer (hint: it's likely not the first suspect), then they/we find out who actually did it (resolution). We have a moment of closing, and finally, we see a list of names nobody reads (after Dick Wolf). Movies, books, and even sitcoms follow this same basic structure. With few exceptions (I'm looking at you *Indiana Jones and the Kingdom of the Crystal Skull*), the stories we consume as entertainment neatly resolve with a happily ever after ending, or at least take us somewhere that leaves us satisfied.

Unfortunately, most of us have lived long enough to understand that life doesn't follow a neat story arc. My final piece of advice for you is this: Don't put a bow on it. To live is to struggle. Even though Rachael, Luke, Sam, and I are in a much better place than we were in the past, and even though we know joy, we also know that more trials and hardships await. I don't even want to think about my boys hitting puberty! But if our journey has taught us anything, it's that we can endure everything if we go through it with God, his people, and the promise that one day Jesus will make all things new, and that includes every broken heart.

Epilogue

~

While I was writing this manuscript, Luke came over to where I was working and asked what I was doing. I told him I was writing a story. He promptly wanted to write a story too, so I typed the following while he dictated it. Without further ado, I present to you a Lucas H. Chisholm original:

Once upon a time, there were two kids. Their names were Luke and Sam, and they wanted to go to Bug City. It's a city where there are all kinds of bugs. Luke and Sam were excited to see Bug City, and then they wanted to go. I said, "We can go to Bug Castle. It's a castle where there's bugs on it." Then, when they got to Bug Castle, it was closed! So, they used a magic key to open the door, and then they said, "Abracadabra!" And the door opened, and they went into Bug World, and they were so excited to go to Bug City, and they were seeing lots of bugs. The end.

(Luke, aged 9 years and 17 days)

Acknowledgments

I can't say thank you enough to my wife, Rachael. Rachael is an amazing wife and mother who has walked through our journey with grace and poise and whose faith puts mine to shame. Thank you for everything that you do, and for being an amazing partner. Thank you also for putting up with the time I spent working on this when I probably should have been helping you with the kids.

One group who never gets enough praise are the nurses, techs, specialists, doctors and other hospital personnel who work long hours, put up with pushy, emotional families, and do the hard work no one else could do. I won't name any of them personally for fear of leaving someone out, but I LOVE the people who work at Medical City Children's Hospital, Children's Medical Center Dallas, Our Children's House at Baylor, Children's Healthcare of Atlanta, and all the therapists' offices, clinics, and other places that literally saved my son's life and helped him exceed all our expectations. To anyone who works with special children, thank you.

I will forever be grateful to the people of the Rockwall and Brin Church of Christ who were the hands and feet of Jesus to us through the most difficult days of our lives. I know that it was the prayers of these Christians, and others across the country, that sustained us and made Luke's life possible. I am also thankful to the Gwinnett Church of Christ for embracing a special needs family and allowing me to be your preacher.

Thanks to my sisters, Rachel and Rebekah, for giving me initial feedback on early drafts of chapters. Thanks to my intern, McKinzy Kendall, for reading the first full draft of this (even though I didn't give him a choice). Thanks to Wayne Joiner for working on the cover design. And thanks to Sonya Armentrout and Titus Custer for listening to me read sections of this to them at the office, and then telling me things like, "Um, you can't say that." And of course, thank you to Luke's grandparents, Gigi and Guapo, and Nana and Papa, who held our hands every step of the way.

A special thanks to my editor, Paula Updegrave, who kindly taught me things like "Commas have rules. You can't just put them wherever." "You can't use the word 'just' in *every* sentence," and, "I think I know what you're trying to say here, but this doesn't make any sense." I know that many grammatical mistakes and made-up words still exist in this book, but I guarantee you that on each one, Paula suggested I fix it, and then I stubbornly insisted on doing it my way. All that to say, any errors herein are solely my own fault.

Acknowledgments

A final special shout out for any courageous child who's ever lived with special needs or medical fragility. You are the real heroes.

Blessings,
DC

If you'd like to connect with me, you can interact on Twitter@_davidhchisholm or by email, davidhchisholm@gmail.com (don't forget the "h" middle initial. I don't know who has davidchisholm@gmail, but he gets a *lot* of my mail). Seriously, let me hear from you! (Unless you hated the book, in which case, my email does NOT include my middle initial.)

One picture of Luke and Sam just because it's my book, and I can do what I want to.

About the Author

David Chisholm is the senior pulpit minister of the Gwinnett Church of Christ in suburban Atlanta, Georgia where he has ministered since 2013. In 2017 he earned a Doctorate of Ministry degree in which he focused on discipleship to help facilitate his passion of helping people in the local church become more like Jesus. He enjoys simple things like hot coffee, college football (Boomer Sooner), good books (preferably science fiction/fantasy if it's not a book on ministry and theology), a solid game on his Xbox, and playing at the park with his sons. He and his wife, Rachael, have two sons: Luke, who is the star of the book, and Sam, Luke's younger brother who thinks he's the star of everything else.

Made in the USA
Coppell, TX
08 August 2020